RESETTING THE JEWEL IN THE CROWN

Expanded edition, featuring an action plan for rebuilding the Indian economy

Solomon Darwin
with Yashraj Bhardwaj

Peaceful Evolution Publishing

Resetting the Jewel in the Crown:
Expanded edition, featuring an action plan for rebuilding the Indian economy

Paperback ISBN: 978-1-7367146-0-7

eBook ISBN: 978-1-7367146-1-4

Editor: Jon Zilber
Book interior layout and cover art design: YouTbooks.com

References to website URLs were accurate at the time of writing. The authors are not responsible for URLs that have changed or expired since the manuscript was prepared.

This book is dedicated to the efforts of the Self-Reliant India goal set by the Honorable Prime Minister Modi and to the 600 million aspirational Indian youth representing the emerging talent of the world who will make the proposed Rebuilding India Initiative a reality.

Shivaji Maharaj

CONTENTS

A NOTE ON
THE EXPANDED EDITION

In 2023, this new edition was published to answer many of the questions outlined in the initial 2020 edition of the book. Those questions were crystallized at the 2022 Berkeley Innovation Forum held in India, chaired by Dr. Rajiv Kumar, Vice Chairman of the NITI Aayog, the planning commission of India. In subsequent research, one-on-one conversations, and – especially – in structured sessions conducted at the 2022 Berkeley Innovation Forum with the participation of dozens of expert representatives from business, government, and academia, a consensus about the answers to many of these questions emerged. This new volume includes those answers.

This combination of purposefully articulated questions and a roadmap for action based on the prevailing consensus about the answers to those questions are provided in two distinct sections. The first was written as the global COVID crisis was ushering in a variety of new uncertainties for the global economy; we've chosen to retain the perspective of that moment in time, as it informs and colors many of the inputs we received at the time.

The new section was completed in 2023. At that point, the lingering aftermath of the COVID crisis, supply chain disruptions, and the resulting economic turmoil were still significant trends shaping the global economy, but there was less uncertainty about the short-term future. As a result, you'll notice a distinct shift in the tone in the second section.

FOREWORD

Henry Chesbrough

UC Berkeley and Luiss University, Rome, Italy

THE PURSUIT OF knowledge is as old as the human race, but the institutions that promoted scientific discovery really arose with the Enlightenment. Before that, there were some individual scientists sponsored by wealthy patrons, as well as the formation of the early universities. But the former had strong incentives to hoard their knowledge, and the latter focused most of their intellectual energy on the liberal arts (divinity being the leading degree conferred by these universities during the Middle Ages).

During the Enlightenment, however, there was something of a Cambrian explosion in scientific institutions that both generated new knowledge and disseminated that knowledge, as the pursuit of knowledge migrated from royal patrons to a much larger merchant class. This migration drove a tremendous increase in both the volume of scientific knowledge generated and in the speed with which new discoveries diffused within society. One landmark event was the formation of the Royal Society in England in 1660, which published its *Philosophical Transactions of the Royal Society* starting in 1665. Similar societies soon emerged in France (1666), Berlin (1700), Russia (1724), and Sweden (1739). By 1700, there were over thirty scientific journals being published, a number that would skyrocket to more than 1,000 journals a century later.

By the 19th century, the scientific method had been established, creating a methodology for more objective investigation into physical and natural phenomena. As the quality of the science improved, the level of trust in that science also rose. Peer review became a widely established practice among scientific journals; all published work would first be judged worthy of publication by disinterested, knowledgeable observers, usually other scientists.

In the 21st century, open-source software has dramatically risen in importance; users of the code can inspect the actual source code that they are using. This radical transparency, along with the ability to make corrections, revisions, and extensions to the code, further enhances the trust and confidence that users can have in the software they use.

As India seeks to accelerate its innovative agenda and "reset the jewel in the crown," questions of innovation, knowledge flows, scientific inquiry and, yes, trust, rise to the fore. This book investigates the opportunities available to India from multiple vantage points, and finds that, if open innovation principles are followed, a promising agenda awaits the country. All of us know more than any of us individually, but it will take sharing, collaboration, and trust to harvest the fruits of innovation in Indian society. This book can provide a map for the journey.

Berkeley, California

REBUILDING INDIA

*"We can't change the direction of the wind,
but we can adjust the sails."*

*– Proverb variously attributed to The Sailors' Prayer Book
and the Reverend Thomas Sheridan*

AS THE "JEWEL in the Crown" of the British Empire, India's stature in the 19th century was without parallel. The British Empire dominated the global economy, and India was the glimmering gem of that empire.

India was a magnet for trade, culture, and ideas, an enchanting subcontinent drawing merchants from various trade routes from the four corners of the world. India held a vast storehouse of natural assets, but the real value of India was its people – brilliant scientists, mathematicians, astronomers, architects, entertainers, and musicians. Queen Victoria, the Empress of India, believed that while the sun never set on the empire, it reflected most brightly on India.

This multi-cultured welcoming community endowed with natural assets attracted explorers and innovators from all over the world. Yet the heart of India could be found in its devotion to its families, communities, and many deities.

Of course, India was a dominant force in the world economy long before there was even a British Empire. The country accounted for more than 38% of global GDP from AD 1 to AD 1000. King Solomon traded with India through peaceful exchange and collaboration. Later, Romans generated as much as 36% of their import tax revenue from Indian goods. Abundant raw materials, rare spices, precious stones, and silver and gold were all part of India's trade network. Ships came to India – the foremost global trade hub of the ancient world – from as far away as Israel, Syria, Egypt, and Greece.

Turning the clock back ever further, the glorious history of India begins with the birth of the Indus Valley Civilization, a highly developed society that flourished in this region around 2,500 BC.

The Indus Valley was home to the largest of the four ancient urban civilizations (Egypt, Mesopotamia, India, and China). They lived in well-planned and well-built towns, which were also centers for trade. They had wide roads and a well-developed drainage system. The houses were made of baked bricks and had two or more levels. The ruins show that these were magnificent merchant cities – well planned, scientifically laid out, and containing architectural marvels that incorporated perfect right angles and perfect circular structures when compared to the inferior structures that were built by later civilizations or invaders. The original settlers did all the necessary math and planning in their heads without the aid of instruments.

But as has happened with all empires, India's position as a global power has risen and fallen. Today, India's position in the world economy is a decidedly mixed bag. On matters of raw scale, India's GDP and population are vast. India's talent pool in many advanced technologies leads the world. And unlike other dominant economies in today's world, India has a reputation for competing hard but always playing fair and respecting the laws, cultures, and traditions of other countries.

India has also excelled at creating and reinventing business models that create value for others while also capturing value for itself to survive and grow. India created value for nations and empires that came from far and near to drink from its well. But it hasn't always captured enough of the value for itself to ensure its own sustainable growth so that it could continue to bless the world even more abundantly.

As a result, India has fallen behind other countries as a global trading center, and as a hub for global investment.

The goal of this book is to provide a roadmap for rebuilding India, by becoming the manufacturing hub for the world. It aims to provide some of the context behind the Rebuilding India Initiative of the Center for Growth Markets at the Haas School of Business at the University of California, Berkeley. The program explores different business models that will benefit all of the stakeholders involved in this process while allowing India to provide a blessing to the nations and people of the world.

India may not be able to replace China's economic role in the global economy anytime soon, but India can aspire to become the most desirable location for companies and countries that value the benefits that India has to offer: An enormous talent pool, much of it English-speaking (more than 12% of the population, compared with less than 1% for China) and much of it tech-savvy. A diverse infrastructure that mixes urban and rural options, and has demonstrated an ability to adapt over its long history. Long-standing relationships with the Western Hemisphere, and an unshakeable respect for the laws, customs, traditions, and norms found outside its own borders.

To clarify the purpose of this book, the goal is to provide a detailed outline for achieving the first step toward that goal. It's a step that's simple to describe, but more complex than it might sound: We need to learn to trust.

What does that mean? Accomplishing an ambitious goal like rebuilding India requires the cooperation of four groups of stakeholders: industry, government, customers, and academia. It would be far more difficult – perhaps impossible – to achieve this goal without the vigorous participation of all four of these groups. But while each of these groups has been able to thrive within its own silo, the level of trust across these groups has eroded in recent years. Industry may not trust government entities to represent their interests. Customers don't necessarily trust businesses. Academics are sometimes viewed as interlopers by other stakeholder groups.

This book focuses on a simple first step that these stakeholder groups can take to reestablish trust among each other: Asking questions. We'll discuss why this is important shortly, and will provide a comprehensive list of questions to help you take part in this initial process.

But before diving into the details, let's return to the historical view to see what we can learn by reviewing the rise and fall of other empires.

The historian Alexander Fraser Tytler (1747-1813) observed that "the average age of the world's greatest civilizations has been 200 years. These nations have progressed through this sequence: From bondage to spiritual faith; From spiritual faith to great courage; From courage to liberty; From liberty to abundance; From abundance to selfishness; From selfishness to apathy; From apathy to dependence; From dependence back into bondage." (He also observed that "a democracy cannot exist as a permanent form of government. It can only exist until the voters discover that they can vote themselves largesse from the public treasury. From that moment on, the majority always votes for the candidates promising the most benefits from the public treasury with the result that a democracy always collapses over loose fiscal policy, always followed by a dictatorship.")

In other words, the ebb and flow of empires is a predictable cycle that follows predictable patterns. (Or, as a lyric from the musical *Hamilton* more succinctly puts it: "Oceans rise, empires fall.")

What spurs the rise of an empire? History provides several reasons behind the meteoric rise of empires over the ages:

- Civilizations engage in active conquest of lands beyond their borders, as seen with Greece, Rome, and Britain
- A charismatic leader, such as Caesar Augustus, Alexander the Great, and Queen Victoria, rallies the society to expand
- A society becomes organized to achieve a specific objective with a unified focus on that goal
- Trade and commerce drive the creation of wealth
- Innovation and cutting-edge technology allow one society to overtake their enemies

And what triggers the demise of an empire?

- The death or loss of a charismatic or visionary leader, without a succession strategy in place
- The unifying vision falls out of focus, or loses a central authority to orchestrate its implementation
- Success breeds complacency, allowing more motivated underdogs to usurp the dominant society
- Corruption and loss of moral values create inequity and a chasm between the rich and the poor, with the latter group rising up in protest
- The converse – adherence to moral values in an immoral world – can also undermine an empire
- Ethnic tensions among a diverse population within an expanded empire
- Failure to innovate or to maintain a technological advantage

Many issues we may think of as contemporary ones – such as the need for sustainable resource management – have actually been threats to society throughout history, as Jeremy Rifkin has outlined in his book *The Empathic Civilization*. For example, in the Roman Empire, forests were over-harvested for their timber. Although this generated short-term profits, this poor stewardship of natural assets soon led to the erosion of the topsoil layer needed to maintain arable land. This in turn led to an inability to support the growing army which drove a spike in taxation. With the economy suffering, there were inadequate investments in technology that might have provided a solution. Efforts to sustain a rapport with the populace were also set aside, opening the doors for internal conflict.

It's often said that those who ignore history are doomed to repeat it. But, ironically, the more attention you pay to history, it also becomes clear that everything will cycle and repeat anyway. But for the moment, we'll stay focused on the present and the foreseeable future. And the question we're focused on is how to rebuild India.

The notion of resetting the jewel in the crown may be a mixed metaphor given that the British Empire is now a shadow of its former self, but there is still a clear path to restoring India's position in the global economy. And the path starts with relearning a crucial skill: How to trust one another.

REBUILDING TRUST

"Trust is the glue of life. It's the most essential ingredient in effective communication. It's the foundational principle that holds all relationships."

– Stephen Covey

EVERYTHING BEGINS WITH trust.

This book is designed to accelerate the ambitious goal of helping India become one of the world's top global manufacturing hubs. A pivotal incident in my professional career sparked the idea that evolved into this book, and that idea was all about the issue of trust.

Or, to be more specific, about the issue of lack of trust.

The lack of trust has been one of the biggest impediments to achieving this lofty goal for India – and for other countries with parallel ambitions. The lack of trust has led many companies to choose to not make the kinds of investments in India that they otherwise might have. Many global brands, emerging tech start-ups, and small entrepreneurial companies have all chosen to make investments elsewhere.

This is despite the fact that India is not only an important market, and a vital manufacturing center on a path to becoming the second-most important manufacturing hub, but it also presents a unique learning opportunity and laboratory for experimentation.

India is the right place to learn about what can work elsewhere. India may have a long and storied history, but it's also a baby country birthed in 1947, younger than America and possessing a young population.

There are many other reasons why India is a great laboratory to experiment in:

- India is in the right place in its lifecycle to embrace new ideas.

- As you rebuild India, you're rebuilding Europe and other areas that are looking to India for talent, resources, and secondary manufacturing hubs beyond China.
- Companies around the world want to expand their markets in India, making it the second-largest industrial hub, because it has an enormous English-speaking and tech-savvy population full of bright and ambitious workers, and has a long tradition of working closely with the West and respecting its laws and culture.

But as I mentioned, many companies are choosing to take a pass on making major investments in India. And a big part of the reason for this has to do with the lack of trust.

Leraning to Trust: Lessons for a Global Reset
I began to think about the nature of trust when I was part of a meeting convened by India's Prime Minister Narendra Modi in October of 2020. The topic was to explore different ways India could accomplish the goal of becoming the world's second manufacturing hub, following the example set by China. In many regards, India was even better suited for this role: The country boasts a long history of relationships with other countries, an educated workforce, robust transportation and other infrastructure, sophisticated technology and technologists, a tradition of respecting the laws and cultures of other countries, and many other attributes that make India a natural manufacturing partner.

Much of the conversation at the meeting called by the Honorable Prime Minister Modi was exactly what one might expect from a diverse group of fifteen experts from around the globe invited to share their perspectives.

Until, that is, one gentleman spoke up. That gentleman had a very simple question for the prime minister: Why doesn't anybody in India trust anybody else?

This was not the sort of question the prime minister was accustomed to receiving. Nor was it the kind of question anybody else in the room was accustomed to hearing at a gathering of this kind. And it didn't receive an especially robust answer at that time.

But it planted a seed.

And that seed grew into this book. (And more, as I'll discuss in a moment.)

What Is Trust?

Before unpacking exactly what I took away from this comment about the lack of trust, let's take a few minutes to first think about the central role that trust plays in our lives, even if it's something many of us don't think about that much.

To truly appreciate the importance of trust in our lives, you need to appreciate that:

- Transactions in our daily life only function because we choose to trust the people and the system behind the transactions
- Every relationship with other people involves a degree of trust, even if it's with somebody we don't think we really trust
- Despite the importance of trust in our lives, we hardly pay any attention to it

The Heart of All Transactions

It's easy to ignore the importance of trust in our society. In fact, many people discount the value of trust entirely. Or worse – they view trust as a liability rather than as an asset. They view people who trust other people as weak; trust is a character flaw. They make no distinction between the willingness to trust others and the gullibility to be taken in by others.

But when you take a close look at our daily life – from our individual interactions with other people to the way governments interact with one another – trust is an essential part of the fabric of every aspect of our society.

Consider, for example, money. In modern times, we've largely abandoned the notion of conducting business by exchanging items of actual value. There was a time when I might trade you a sheep for some woven goods, or an apple pie in exchange for an hour of your labor. Today, one party typically is willing to part with some item of obvious value – goods or services – in exchange for something that has absolutely no obvious value, something which is merely a piece of paper (currency, or a check) or some coins or some kind of digital currency.

These completely lopsided transactions – valuable goods and services in exchange for mere symbols of value – are only possible in a society that places an extraordinary degree of trust in the concept of money. Indeed, in many financial transactions, neither party is offering anything of tangible value; both sides are offering up one kind of stand-in for value (perhaps cash) for some other kind of stand-in for value (perhaps stock).

But it doesn't stop there. Our exchange of cash for stock probably doesn't even involve an actual exchange of cash for stock. It often is merely a digital representation of cash (a digital funds transfer) in exchange for a digital representation of stock (from an online broker).

If you dig even deeper into this highly abstract transaction, there may be something tangible lurking at the end of a series of exchanges and conversions. For example, back when many currencies operated on the gold standard, the government issuing the currency could, in theory, convert all of the currency in circulation into gold, should the need arise. But what gives gold any value? Aside from the occasional industrial applications for gold, the value of gold is largely an artificial construct. You can't eat it, you can't use it to keep yourself warm. Many find it aesthetically pleasing, but many also find other nearly worthless materials to be equally aesthetically pleasing. The value of gold, or of the compressed form of coal known as diamonds, only exists because various parties long ago were able to create a system of trust around it.

What else, besides money, is based on trust? The notion of ownership of land is related to a variety of documents such as deeds. Unlike money, land actually has some intrinsic value. You can live on it, you can farm on it, you can find treasure under the surface of it. It's real, as the term "real estate" suggests.

But our transactions involving real estate are also built on a foundation of trust. If I want to buy some property from you, I need to be able to trust that there are no competing claims to the title for the land. I must trust that surveyors marked off the boundaries of the land accurately. I need to determine if there are any creditors that you've already sold (or lent, in the form of a mortgage) the land to.

The Basis of All Relationships
What else, beyond the transactional world, is based on a foundation of trust? Personal relationships. We agree to share our lives, our vulnerabilities, and our dreams with those close to us. That would be much less common without mutual trust.

We vote for elected officials and (at least until recently) rarely, if ever, questioned whether the candidates with the most votes were properly declared the victors.

This kind of social capital is a more powerful force than financial capital for building a community or a nation. I have seen this happen in rural India working with the smart village movement. Whenever we launched our smart village programs, many women came out to attend with their cell phones in their hands. They banded together to get things done as a group through text messages and making their requests known to the local government officials who gave them deaf ears in the past.

In the past, these women had grown accustomed to not having their voices heard, even after waiting in long lines in the sun in front of government offices. Now government officials come running to them when they make a call; they need the votes of these women. Using their cell phones as the backbone of their community, these poor rural women now have political power; they can vote officials out of office.

Perhaps even more astonishing is the degree of trust we place in caretakers. We agree to allow doctors to inject us with drugs. We send our children off to schools every day to be cared for by teachers we might never even have met. We also allow our children to be indoctrinated by lessons that we might have never seen but which we are increasingly discovering include questionable accounts of history and other subjects.

In a very real sense, we trust a variety of people with our most scarce and most precious resource of all: Our time. We empower others to create art for us to enjoy – books, music, plays, TV shows, movies – and willingly offer up many hours every day to consume their output. We may sometimes be disappointed by what we experience, but most people continue to come back for more, again and again. Even if it isn't earned, we continue to trust that there's at least the possibility that maybe there will be something good on TV tonight.

The Invisible Foundation
If you haven't thought about the role of trust in these aspects of human endeavor before, this may come as a bit of a surprise. But what's even more surprising – given the way trust shapes so many different activities – is how little we think about it.

It's not part of the standard academic curriculum.

The understanding of trust is not a well-defined discipline.

There are few practical handbooks for building trust, or for determining when there is no basis for trust. Theater and improv students may do trust exercises and marriage counselors may help couples establish deeper trust. But are parents trained on how to detect untrustworthy teachers? Do MBAs routinely learn how to think about trust as an essential part of virtually every transaction?

The concept of open innovation provides a good example of how changing the way we think about trust in our business relationships can make a powerful and measurable difference. UC Berkeley professor Henry Chesbrough, the father of open innovation, explains the concept by observing the benefit of having knowledge acquired or created by humans flow both from and into an organization to accelerate solutions. Closed Vs. Open innovation on next page.

Closed Innovation Funnel
Value is Created but is not Captured
Unshared Knowledge is Useless

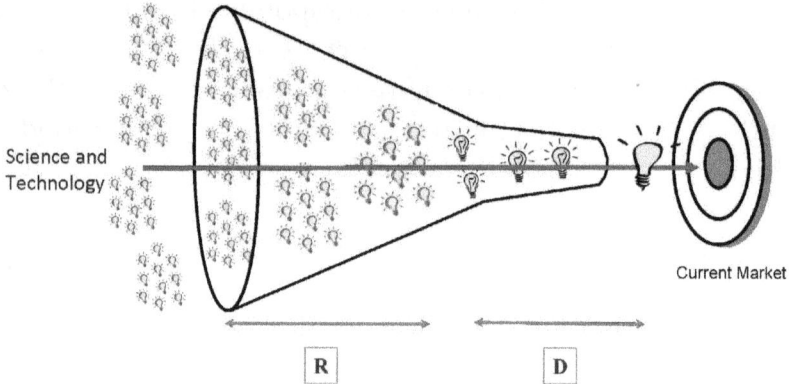

Science and Technology

Current Market

R

D

Open Innovation Funnel
Knowledge Flows like a River in all directions to Accelerate Solutions

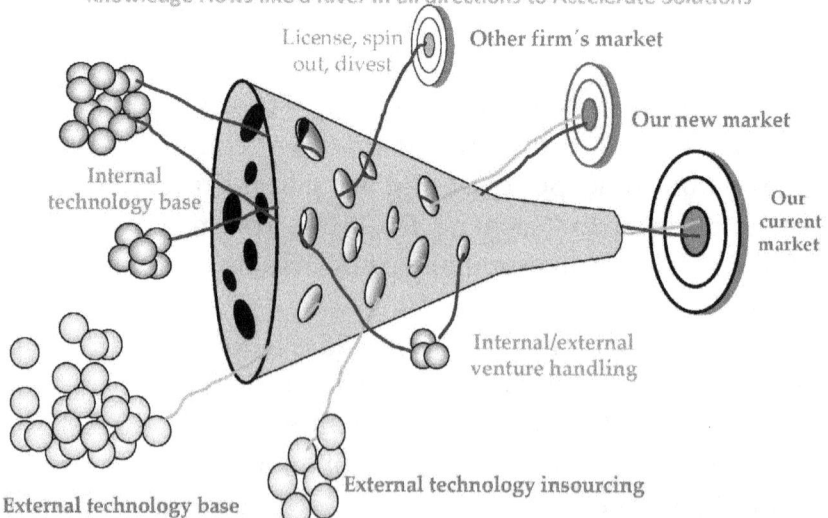

License, spin out, divest

Other firm's market

Our new market

Internal technology base

Our current market

Internal/external venture handling

External technology insourcing

External technology base

Slide Source: Henry Chesbrough

Closed Innovation Story
Unutilized Knowledge Laid Waste for 10 years

1948: Transistor was Invented at AT&T Bell Labs
Hidden in the knowledge lake due to greed

1958: Transistor Radio introduced by Sony at $39 to bless
the world after 10 years to closed innovation.

Open Innovation Story

iPod idea came from
Tony Fadell, an engineer at
Phillips

Phillips Rejects the Idea

Tony Fadell Collaborates
With many firms through
Open Innovation
- Apple
- Texas Instruments
- Toshiba
- Portal Player
- Wolfson
- Many Others Firms

Took only
9 months!
With Open
Innovation
From Start to
Finish

Takeaway: Open Innovation Accelerates Solutions to Society
10 years (Transistor Radio) vs 9 months (iPod –through open Innovation)

Without barriers, open innovation creates frictionless platforms that facilitate access to global markets, ultimately enriching all stakeholders. His research provides many examples in which open innovation has accelerated knowledge and enabled technologies to be leveraged to provide superior and timely solutions.

Our species' collective knowledge grows every day. But when it is simply stored in isolation, like a lake, it stagnates. To serve a useful purpose, it must flow like a river.

Business models based on such knowledge flows have been demonstrated to be both scalable and sustainable. Our Rebuilding India Initiative is based on open innovation principles and strategies to accelerate solutions that resolve specific pain points.

How Do You Rebuild Trust?
After thinking about that meeting with the prime minister, I came to realize that the lack of strong, trusting relationships was a key problem – and quite likely, *the* fundamental barrier – holding India back from achieving this vision of reclaiming its role as a preeminent economic force in the world.

Now, when I refer to the lack of strong, trusting relationships, I don't mean that it would be great if everybody just automatically believed everybody else. That's gullibility, not trust. Trust means that you're at least open to the possibility that the other parties are sharing accurate (and demonstrably accurate) information, and that while you may differ on some aspects of some goals, you likely agree on other aspects of other goals.

Consider a simple example of a business transaction based on trust. I would like to sell you a sweater that I've knitted for $50.

There is generally information that each party knows that the other party doesn't. I might know that I'm willing to lower my price to $40, and you might know you're willing to pay as much as $60. Perhaps you know that you also plan to buy a dozen more sweaters later this year,

One of us may wind up feeling they got a "better deal." If I was prepared to lower my price to $40 and sold it for $45, I may feel I did well. You might have gotten a purchase price lower than you were willing to pay, and might also feel you did well. Or you may feel like you paid more than you should have, but did it anyway because you felt pressured to have a gift for your spouse.

Perhaps you share with me the fact that you will be looking to buy 12 more sweaters soon. I may be willing to sell you this sweater for less than the $40 minimum price that I have in my head because I feel like it's a good investment toward future revenues.

At no point in this transaction is either of us lying. At no point in this transaction do we suspect the other of cheating or misrepresenting anything. We may only care about this one-time transaction, or we may be thinking about an ongoing relationship. Or perhaps one of us may be thinking about a one-time transaction while the other is thinking about an ongoing relationship.

We can engage in this kind of negotiation and transaction when there's trust about the fundamentals. Neither of us suspects the other of fraudulent behavior. I don't think you're passing off counterfeit money or paying with a stolen credit card, and you don't harbor suspicions that I'm selling you hot goods. We trust each other, even though we are in many ways adversaries in a business negotiation. I hope to come out as well as I can at the end of the process, as do you – but not by fleecing you, or by misrepresenting my wares.

Of course, if one of us *does* act in a fraudulent manner (and is caught doing so), our relationship will crumble. But most of the time, in most of our interactions, we're able to operate based on a solid foundation of trust. We may be business adversaries, political opponents, academic rivals, or shoppers fighting tooth and nail among each other for the last available PlayStation 5 on Black Friday. But those types of competitive attitudes don't threaten the fundamental trust that allows us to successfully operate together. We may not always cooperate among ourselves, but we can nonetheless do business together.

This kind of trust permeates the fabric of our everyday life. As consumers, it makes commerce simple and nearly frictionless. As participants in civil society, it makes for stable governments. As businesspeople, it allows different companies to work together. As academics and researchers, it promotes the expansion of knowledge.

Trust is everywhere.

Except, apparently, in the room where it happened with Prime Minister Modi.

So what prompted the question to Prime Minister Modi? And what prompted those gathered at the meeting to collectively (if silently) gasp in acknowledgement of the truth of the question?

Generally speaking, there is trust among a group of the same type of stakeholders. Consumers trust consumers. Business people trust other businesses. Government officials trust their counterparts. And academics tend to assume that other academics are playing fairly, regardless of rivalries or competition among them.

But the attitudes *across* different stakeholder groups are very different.

Do consumers trust their government? Rarely.

Do government leaders trust academics? Sadly, no.

Do academics feel that industry executives can be counted on to act responsibly? Not often.

How do industry leaders feel about their customers? There's little trust, and abundant skepticism.

Within each stakeholder group, there is a sufficient level of trust for daily life to transpire in a productive manner, in all the arenas I mentioned earlier (commerce, personal relationships, entertainment, and so forth). But when one group looks at the other groups, the trust dissipates and the barriers emerge.

Why is this?

My goal isn't to analyze all of the sociological, psychological, or historical factors at play. How did this level of trust evolve? Which relationships are the least trusting? What factors have occasionally created a thawing of the apprehension among these groups? I'll leave those analyses to others.

What I do feel is essential, though, is that one of the reasons why the level of distrust has grown so high and remains so high is the challenge of communication among these groups. They bring different assumptions, carry different cultural baggage, and speak different languages – figuratively, at least, and sometimes literally.

For example, a government official may be excited about a new program offering industry the financial incentives to upgrade key infrastructure systems, such as warehousing. But the response has been lackluster, and they have no idea why.

Industry leaders may be skeptical because they're drawing comparisons with past programs that went awry. To their way of thinking, not only is this program worthless, but it's *less* than worthless – it's yet another example of how government wastes tax dollars and plays favorites.

Using Questions to Spur Trust

Now, if I was a mediator attempting to reconcile a feud between neighbors demonstrating this degree of mistrust, there are several different approaches I might attempt. Maybe I'd spend time trying to understand each person's background, from childhood to adulthood. Perhaps I'd speak to each of them separately, and then share with the other what their partner had shared with me.

But I'm not a mediator, and anyway, relationships among these stakeholder groups are very different kinds of relationships. But I think the thing I'd try first is to ask each party: What are the questions you have for the other person?

Perhaps these are questions you haven't felt comfortable asking. Perhaps they're questions you've asked dozens of times, and have never gotten a satisfactory answer to them, or an answer that made any sense to you. Perhaps it's never occurred to you that you have some unanswered questions, and that those mysteries might be what's burning a hole in your relationship.

Don't worry – I have no intention of pursuing a new career as a mediator or a relationship therapist. But, in a way, what will follow in this book is an effort to help build better relationships among these key groups of stakeholders. And the strategy is basically as simple as this example I've offered of the neighbors that have very little trust between them.

For this couple, an excellent starting point would be to articulate and raise the questions they have for each other. Ideally, these questions would be rooted in some soul-searching, not just some top-of-mind griping and ranting at each other. Instead, they'd be meaningful questions that, if answered satisfactorily, have the potential to begin to build trust between the two parties.

The answers to the questions may or may not be important. Simply asking the questions may be enough to begin to establish some trust. Asking the question – and listening to the questions being asked of you – means that communication is happening. And communication is the first step toward building trust.

Is that first step – asking the essential questions that have been troubling you, and seeing evidence that the other party has heard and understood the question, and understands why the question is important to you – is that first step enough?

Well, at this point, I'm going to stop pretending to know anything about being a mediator and speak more directly to my true topic: Is it enough for the four stakeholder groups I've mentioned to begin to have a dialogue among each other, or does there need to be the resolution of clear and unambiguous answers to everybody's questions for one another?

My answer is: I don't know. But I'm confident that if these four groups could engage in a more robust and more trusting dialogue, we could move closer to the goal of establishing India as the world's second manufacturing hub much more quickly. And I'm also confident that the more we can answer these questions, the faster we can make progress toward that goal.

In this book we're going to catalog a series of questions from each of the four stakeholder groups. We've identified five categories of questions that we think are essential aspects of the process of achieving this goal for India. In each of those categories, we've identified crucial questions *from* each of the stakeholder groups to each of the other three stakeholder groups. (If you're doing the math, that turns out to be a total of 60 lists of questions.)

For most of these questions, we've provided the source for our research – a source you can pursue if you want to explore the topic in more detail, or get a better sense of why we felt it was an important question.

Now, before we dive into the list of questions, I'm going to provide a little context about two things. First, how did we identify the four key groups of stakeholders? And second, how did we identify the five key topics to address in our list of questions?

The goal of establishing India as a global manufacturing hub on a par with China is hardly a new idea. It's been discussed for many years. And in the wake of the COVID-19 pandemic, many business leaders have expanded the topic into a framework for "rebuilding India" once the immediate risks have been contained and mitigated (as most public health officials believe they will be). In August of 2020, senior executives from 40 leading global companies took part in a Berkeley Innovation Forum India (BIFI) that I hosted in my capacity as Executive Director for the Center for

Growth Markets at the Haas School of Business. (See complete list of companies in Appendix 1.)

This group (chaired by Amitabh Kant, CEO of NITI Aayog and Sunil Munjal, the Chairman of Hero Enterprise) was the largest gathering of representatives of leading corporate voices joining together with the shared goal of driving the Indian economy forward through collaboration. The participants attending that online gathering – including senior executives from such companies as Ericsson, IBM, Intel, Oracle, Salesforce, SAP, TATA, TechMahindra, and Wipro – articulated their goals as identifying opportunities to enhance and develop scalable and sustainable opportunities to collaborate on value chains and other elements of a mutually beneficial ecosystem.

More specifically, the attendees sought to:

- Reduce or eliminate costs
- Mitigate risks through collaborative action
- Remove or relieve bottlenecks
- Reinforce weak links in their processes
- Identify mutually beneficial opportunities to share resources.

Those "bottom-up" tactics would help drive the "top down" objectives for India as a whole, namely to:

- Establish the country as the second global manufacturing hub for diversified global supply chains
- Develop digital infrastructure for early education and skill development that will bolster job creation and create and sustain a talent pipeline

- Create essential ecosystems in key sectors of the economy to mitigate the lingering risks resulting from the pandemic, encompassing:
  - Efficient "last-mile" healthcare solutions
  - Transparent agriculture platforms that yield frictionless farm-to-plate channels
  - Policies that promote financial inclusion and risk mitigation in underserved sectors and regions

The range and diversity of participants in this three-day conversation provided several different lenses through which to view these topics. For example, many contributors emphasized the factors that were needed to successfully transform these goals into reality. These included:

- Accelerating digital transformation to leverage the increasingly interconnected nature of our world
- Stimulating internal and external creativity through open innovation
- Creating and expanding ecosystems to share risks, costs, and resources
- Striving to remain adaptable by challenging and changing organizations and mindsets
- Diversifying in effective and efficient ways, often by identifying "minimum viable ecosystems" (a topic I'll expand on shortly)

Each of these factors by itself will require further dialogue to develop workable action plans for specific industries. But certain themes common to nearly all industries and most stakeholders also emerged. In particular, there was a clear need to establish greater trust among different groups of stakeholders so that they could foster stronger working relationships.

Consider how the idea of trust supports and enhances several of the factors just mentioned:

– Accelerating digital transformation: Without trust, new opportunities fail to materialize (or take much longer to do so) regardless of the technologically interconnected nature of our society. The only things that accelerate are skepticism and suspicions.

– Creativity through open innovation: Trust resides at the heart of the concept of open innovation, a system based on the principle of freely sharing ideas. Where trust is limited or nonexistent, few organizations will be willing to freely offer up their own ideas to others without confidence that the other organizations will reciprocate.

– Similarly, ecosystems in which multiple participants share resources to reduce risks and costs can only be effective when those contributing to the ecosystem have firm expectations that they will also benefit from the contributions made by others.

The challenges created by a lack of trust among stakeholders is an extreme version of what is often referred to as "the tragedy of the commons." This concept is derived from the notion that individuals that are solely focused on their own self-interest will often make decisions and take actions that have negative outcomes not just for others but also, ultimately, for themselves. When there is shared land – a commons – that shepherds could use to allow their flocks to graze, there's a temptation for each individual shepherd to let their own flock overgraze (to better fatten them up for market). But this overgrazing not only means that some shepherds will be left without any opportunity for their flocks to graze, but it also makes it more likely that the over-grazed land won't yield much of a harvest in subsequent years. So even the greediest of the shepherds who think they're acting in their own best interest are actually engaging in self-defeating behaviors.

With several groups of stakeholders involved, there are even more threats and risks to the shared resource. Imagine, for example, that a real estate developer decided, on their own, to pave over the commons area to build a shopping mall. With no grazing land available, the shepherds will all relocate to some other area – leaving no customers for the new shopping mall. The shepherds are displaced, and the developer winds up bankrupt.

When trust is part of the fabric of the community, the different stakeholder groups can communicate and find win-win solutions, rather than lose-lose disasters. For example, the shepherds could establish fair and reasonable grazing schedules, including penalties for those who might be tempted to overdo it. The developer could invite the community to weigh in on possible locations for their project, a process that would have surfaced the vital importance of not infringing on the only viable grazing land in the community.

As mentioned earlier, developing this baseline degree of trust in the community doesn't ensure that there won't be the occasional bad actors who violate that trust. But it does mean that there can be norms and expectations for how most people will behave most of the time. And that baseline of trust facilitates, in this example, everything from expectations around access to shared resources to planning processes for community development.

Defining the Goal of Rebuilding India

Looking more closely at the challenge and opportunity for the Indian economy, our working assumption was that the overall objective could be stated as follows:

Build an ecosystem that creates trust that enables
and facilitates scaling and reinvigoration of
the Indian economy

To facilitate and expedite achieving this goal – which some have characterized as part of a "global reset" – it would be essential for those driving the Indian economy to explore new business models that have been successful in other regions and in various industries. For example, subscription models for various goods and services have made huge inroads in many industries. Indeed, in many cases they have completely disrupted well-established business models.

The days of selling software in a box, for example, are largely behind us. More and more people purchase entertainment – movies, music, and TV shows – by subscribing to streaming services, rather than by purchasing physical media. (In fact, many people who watch "TV" don't even own televisions, watching programs only on their phone or tablet.) Other industries have embarked on a path toward "Uberization," making it possible (or, in some cases, mandatory) for their workforce to operate as independent and/or part-time contractors. In some cases, these industries have created new hybrid workforces combining both full-time and "gig" workers, an outcome requiring reinventing many of their established workflows and processes, being driven by economic benefits in some cases or, in other cases, economic necessity.

Even more extreme examples of new business models have arisen in which, for example, long-time capitalist economies (or large sectors of an economy, such as healthcare and education) are exploring alternatives.

Which (if any) of these dramatic changes are applicable to the goal of establishing India as a global manufacturing hub remains an open question. And it will remain a purely hypothetical one until a higher degree of trust is established among the stakeholders. Assuming that a stronger foundation of trust will be established, however, the fundamental objective is to explore and assess new models for a more robust ecosystem.

Learning from Both Success and Failure
How can we quickly absorb the right lessons from what others have already explored? Consider the mottos of two icons of science and technology. From science, Isaac Newton observed about his own accomplishments that "if I have seen further it is by standing on the shoulders of Giants." And from technology, Mark Zuckerberg attributes much of Facebook's success to a philosophy of "failing fast" – that is, test ideas and learn just as much from the ones that don't work out as from the ones that do.

Learn from failures as well as from successes.

Most people are comfortable with Newton's philosophy (even if they're not necessarily as modest). We learn from the successes of those who have gone before us. (Or as the painter Pablo Picasso supposedly said more bluntly, "Good artists borrow, great artists steal.")

The Zuckerberg motto, in contrast, strikes many as counter-intuitive. But it is fundamentally aligned with a basic premise of the scientific method championed by Newton: There are no unsuccessful experiments. Regardless of the outcome, every well-formulated and well-executed experiment adds valuable data that brings us closer to the goal of knowledge. If an experiment proves that the hypothesis is incorrect, it still narrows down the number of hypotheses that remain. The "discovery" of the practical electric light bulb that relied on a tungsten filament could just as easily be described as the discovery of which 999 filament candidates would prove to be impractical.

Failures often provide crucial learnings that help us understand why asking questions and raising topics that are often left buried is so important.

Understanding Stakeholder Concerns

Now that you understand our objective – to explore ideas for developing a scalable and sustainable ecosystem that will rebuild India as a global manufacturing hub – and our approach – to learn from both successes and failures – perhaps it is clear that understanding the questions each stakeholder group has for each of the other stakeholder groups is so critical.

> *Understanding the incentives, interests, and concerns*
> *that different stakeholders have is the first step*
> *in cracking this puzzle.*

There's more than one reason why it's essential to understand the questions each group has for the other groups. The most fundamental one may be the least obvious: It's next to impossible to build trust among the stakeholder groups unless each group is confident that the other groups have heard their concerns. In many cases, simply knowing that their concerns have been heard is more important than whatever answer they might receive.

A key pillar supporting a trusting relationship is knowing that the other party or parties have heard you. That means more than knowing that you've spoken; it means that your input or your question has been acknowledged. (And it also doesn't mean that you've received an answer, or that you're happy with the answer you might have received.)

Knowing that you've been heard is generally a necessary prerequisite behind a trusting relationship. Sometimes stakeholders know that the only answer they can offer won't be one that the other party wants to hear. As a result, they dodge the question or avoid offering any kind of response, even one that simply acknowledges that they've received and understand the question or the perspective being offered.

What's unfortunate in this scenario is that both parties are very nearly fully engaged in a dialogue. They may both understand the concerns of the other party – but just don't want to acknowledge that to each other. The concern is that the lack of a satisfactory answer would lead to frustration. In fact, it's often the lack of an acknowledgement of the other party's position or questions that leads to far greater frustration.

When the relationships among stakeholders are strained (or non-existent), they can't raise questions for one another. That's the rationale behind the catalog of questions we'll soon be sharing: If the stakeholder groups haven't been able to bring themselves to ask these questions to one another, perhaps this book can serve to help break the ice and bootstrap that dialogue. Only once a dialogue has begun can a stronger degree of trust begin to emerge.

Framing the Dialogue

Once the channels for dialogue have been established, there are no limits on what can be accomplished. At our 2020 BIFI event, the attendees generated a wellspring of ideas which were further expanded and refined over the course of three days. Each participant brought their own unique perspective but, loosely speaking, their ideas could be categorized into four categories:

- Moving Beyond Balance Sheets
- Forging Equitable Partnerships Among Governments, Academia, and Business Enterprises
- Fostering the Development of Powerful Ecosystems
- Maintaining a Consistent Flow of Information Through Recurring Information Exchanges

Let's explore some specific ideas, proposals, and examples that illuminate each of these categories.

Moving Beyond Balance Sheets

The modern balance sheet dates back to at least the late 15th century as part of the accounting system outlined by an Italian monk named Luca Pacioli. It has played an important role in facilitating the global spread of commerce, becoming a standard tool used by businesses from mom-and-pop corner stores to multinational corporations. In fact, an earlier book of mine – *How to Think like the CEO of the Planet* – proposed using "the balance sheet of the earth" as a useful tool for restoring the environmental health of the earth.

But as a standard business tool, the balance sheet is no longer quite as universally applicable as it once was. In today's economy, an increasing slice of the working population plays a role that's very different from the traditional full-time (or part-time) employee. So-called "gig" workers may work a full slate of hours with one company paying them, or they may divide their time among several employers. Or they may shift their hours into a schedule quite different from the traditional 40-hour workweek.

For example, a driver might work 10 days on, 10 days off, alternating the pattern to facilitate childcare, eldercare, their own medical conditions, other jobs, their spouse's or partner's job, or perhaps just personal preference. This often involves a pattern of compensation for the workforce that won't make as much sense for an employer using a traditional balance sheet. For a rideshare company like Uber, for example, the company doesn't incur the cost of owning or insuring a fleet of vehicles – they're owned and insured by the drivers – so these expenses will affect the company's finances in a different way than they might have for an old-school taxi company.

For many companies in the so-called sharing economy, the key activity that differentiates them and that determines their success or failure in the market is their arsenal of digital tools and infrastructure. Their most important skills might be their ability to orchestrate and rapidly deploy these soft assets and knowledge resources. Contrast this with their predecessors – such as a traditional taxi company – for which ownership of physical assets (the taxis, taxi medallions) and the wherewithal to perform various services on those assets (such as maintenance, fueling, and the like) were strategically critical assets. It's easy to see how the importance of a balance sheet intended primarily for tracking physical assets with fixed values might no longer be as relevant in an era in which digital assets (with values that can fluctuate wildly) have grown in importance.

**Forging Equitable Partnerships Among Governments,
Academia, and Business Enterprises**

Crafting a partnership is, relatively speaking, easy. Crafting an equitable partnership is something else altogether. What does "equitable" mean in this context? Your dictionary will tell you that equitable is simply a fancy word for "fair." Partnerships that are fair and beneficial to all parties – what are often called win-win relationships – tend to have a stronger impact and last much longer than lopsided partnerships in which one party reaps the lion's share of the benefits.

But your dictionary may also remind you of the root word "equity." Equity suggests something even deeper than just fairness. When you build equity as a result of a partnership, you're creating something that you can own – maybe not in a literal or financial sense, but at a deeper and more emotional sense. A partnership might be fair, but without all parties coming out of that partnership with a sense of equity, they're not really stakeholders; your equity in a relationship is what gives you your stake as a stakeholder.

What does this translate into in practical terms? Consider a typical consumer transaction. You go to a store to buy a gallon of milk. You swipe your credit card, and walk out with your purchase. Presumably, it was a fair transaction – you and the grocer both agreed that the price was appropriate – and represents a very simple partnership between you and the merchant. But neither party really has an equity in this partnership.

And that's not just because the stakes – the dollar amount involved – are so low. Consider a more expensive purchase: you've decided to buy a car. Unlike the purchase of a gallon of milk, there might be a little bit of negotiation involved. But the terms of what's open to negotiation is extremely limited. You might offer a lower purchase price, or insist on a higher valuation for your trade-in. Perhaps you'll demand that the car dealer toss in a set of floor mats.

But the overwhelming majority of the terms of your purchase are non-negotiable. Keep in mind that when you finalize the purchase, both parties will be signing a lengthy contract, with dozens or even hundreds of detailed terms that govern the transaction. It will never even occur to most customers to even question any of those terms (other than the price). And imagine if a customer did try to negotiate some of the terms – for example, perhaps you want to challenge the provision in section 27 of the contract that states that any disputes regarding the purchase will be settled based on the laws of the state in which the car manufacturer is headquartered. The car dealer wouldn't even begin to know how to respond.

In other words, while you might wind up feeling that you got the car for a fair price, you're unlikely to feel that you have any equity in a partnership between you and the car dealer.

Contrast this with the typical practice of negotiating a transaction between two sizable businesses. One side will typically offer a proposed contract, and the other side will often decide to counter that proposal with extensive changes to dozens of the terms laid out in that initial proposal. Everything is on the table. By the time the two parties have arrived at a contract that's mutually agreeable, both sides will feel that they have not merely hammered out an acceptable deal, but they'll likely feel a sense of equity in the relationship between them.

By creating this equity in the relationship, this paves the way for future transactions between the two companies. They'll understand each other's concerns and sensitivities. And they'll have created a template that they can easily clone as the basis for future transactions. Assuming the terms of the deal were acceptable to both sides, both parties will be more likely to do business again with each other rather than try to do business with some unknown and untested potential partner.

An equitable partnership doesn't just mean conducting transactions that both parties consider to be fair; it means both parties have invested time and energy in understanding one another, and have forged a relationship that smooths the way for an ongoing series of future transactions. In other words, the stakeholders have created a path that is forward-looking and scalable.

Applying this notion to the goal of building India into a global manufacturing hub, the broader challenge comes as we think about a more complex matrix of relationships than a simple transaction between a business and a consumer or between two businesses. When you break down the many, many sub-tasks that need to be accomplished to achieve this goal, you'll see that many of them involve stakeholders from different communities.

Businesses generally know how to conduct transactions with other businesses. Government agencies generally know how to conduct transactions with other agencies. And academics know how to work with other academics. But the tasks that are the stepping stones to our goal of rebuilding India often involve businesses working with government, or governments working with academia, or academics working with industry, or all three groups working together.

That's typically a much bigger challenge.

Triple Helix Framework
Knowledge Generation, Deployment & Capture

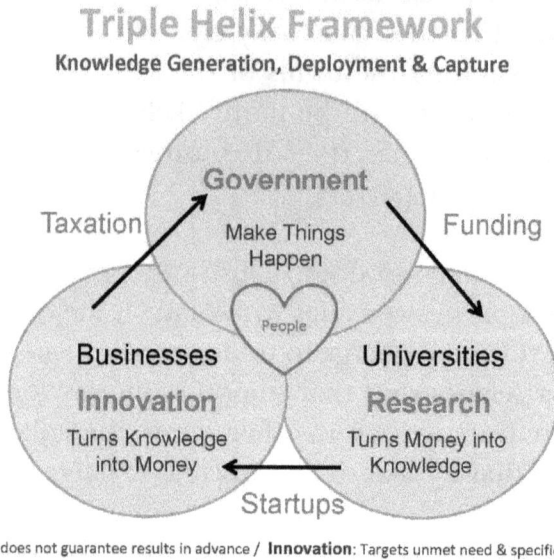

Research: does not guarantee results in advance / **Innovation**: Targets unmet need & specific outcomes

When you look at how change and innovation emerge in a particular industry or in a sector of the economy, there's often a pattern that Henry Etzkowitz of Stanford University has called the Triple Helix Model. In this model, government entities, businesses, and academia form the three strands of the triple helix. Innovation often appears first in academia, where research labs develop ideas that can potentially be applied to a variety of industrial applications. New technologies and startups emerge out of the academic environment and find their way into industry. This helps economies grow and, in turn, generates new and desirable jobs and new tax revenues. The potential of these innovations provides government agencies with incentives to fund academic research, and the cycle becomes self-perpetuating.

Triple Helix Framework
Why it does not work in some countries
Government Policy is the Biggest Barrier to Economic Growth

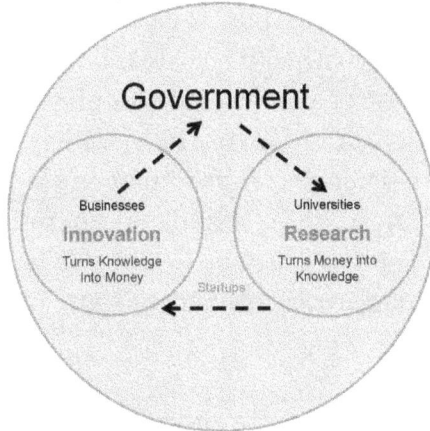

Government

Businesses

Innovation

Turns Knowledge
into Money

Universities

Research

Turns Money into
Knowledge

Startups

Each of the stakeholders represented by the circles need to have a comparable seat at the table for the triple helix to work. In many countries, the role of the government dominates that of the other two stakeholders, and the model fails to live up to its potential. With both positive and negative examples of how the triple helix model has worked or where the conditions for its success weren't met, this model has been well established. For example, in several Silicon Valley industries the model has worked well by building a cycle in which a U.S. government investment resulted in the creation of jobs that yielded revenue from taxpayers, returning the original investment to the government while also creating a substantial ROI to subsequent investors all over the world. (The U.S. Government has often been the first mover to invest in knowledge creation through institutions such as Berkeley and Stanford that created many innovations that made Silicon Valley and other industries possible.)

We are adapting the triple helix model in our work on the Rebuilding India Initiative. In assessing the challenge of rebuilding India, we added a fourth element to the helix: customers. In many economies, customers play a vigorous and active role that shapes and informs the other three stakeholder groups. One reason for this is the critical role that villages play in the Indian economy. Unlike many parts of the world in which urban economies dominate the infrastructure, India's villages are home to 700 million people including millions of entrepreneurs and aspirational entrepreneurs. (The emergence of "smart village" models of innovation for India's villages is the subject of some of my earlier books, including *The Road to Mori*.)

In smart villages and other communities, the role of individual customers or collective groups of customers can play a pivotal role in determining whether economic initiatives succeed or not, wielding an impact on par with that of government, industry, and academia. So our analysis has an expanded scope, essentially becoming an examination of a quadruple helix model.

Fostering the Development of Powerful Ecosystems
An ecosystem builds on the benefits of an equitable partnership and extends and scales it so that it can accommodate a broad range of partners. Rather than hashing out individual agreements with multiple parties, the creation of a comprehensive ecosystem can streamline participation in a new business model, technology, or other transformative innovation.

The Smart Village Movement (SVM) offers a useful example of how a holistic ecosystem can drive innovation and positive outcomes. To illustrate the workings of the SVM ecosystem, we created a series of maps that indicate the journeys that various types of customers (students, patients, farmers, and so forth) will take.

A Student's Journey

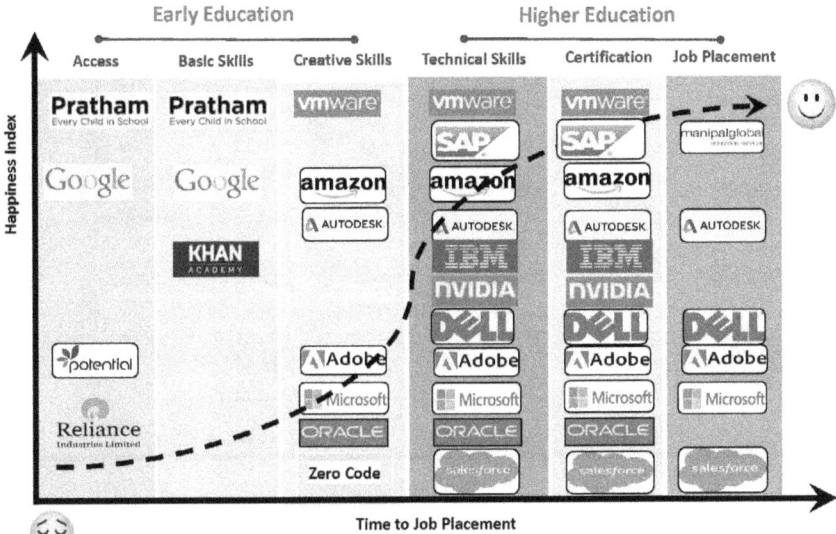

Education: Click Zoom Link to Recordings of Executives Presentations

Value Propositions of Participating Firms
Education & Skill Development

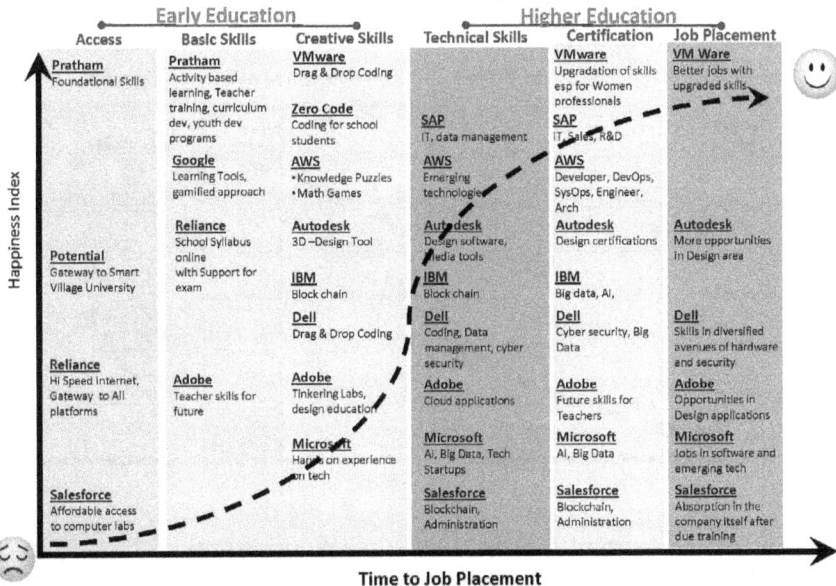

Education: Click Zoom Link to Recordings of Executives Presentations

A Patient's Journey

A Farmer's Journey

Agriculture: Click Zoom Link to Recordings of Executives Presentations

A Household Journey

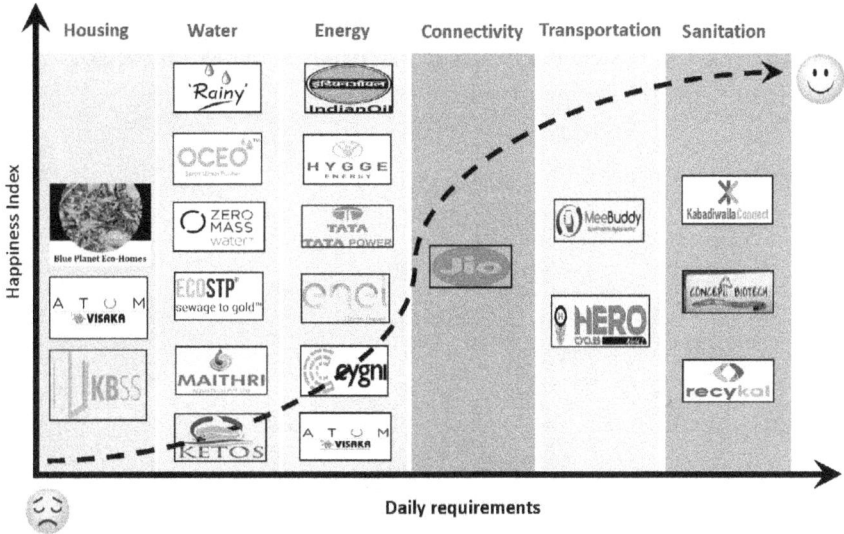

© Solomon Darwin 2020: All Rights Reserved

Like a natural ecosystem such as our human body, a business eco-system has various needs and various resources. Fundamentally, it needs to have a purpose for its existence. It must be well planned to overcome any obstacles so that it can achieve its purpose and work harmoniously to benefit all stakeholders. And it must be sustainably and regularly renewed to be self-reliant as a holistic system.

The Rebuilding India Initiative should be based on a similar ecosystem approach. Our model for the holistic SVM ecosystem highlights key resources that are often essential components of an ecosystem, such as energy and communications. An essential aspect of this kind of model is that it is powered by real-time infor-mation and incorporates mechanisms so that there can be imme-diate flows of communication as different needs arise. Each of the seven hexagonal components in the model should be headed up by a decision maker who can "write the check and take the risk." There must be commitment and a willingness to adapt as each function learns to survive. This is a critical success factor for a low-friction sustainable ecosystem.

SVM Holistic Ecosystem
Participating Companies

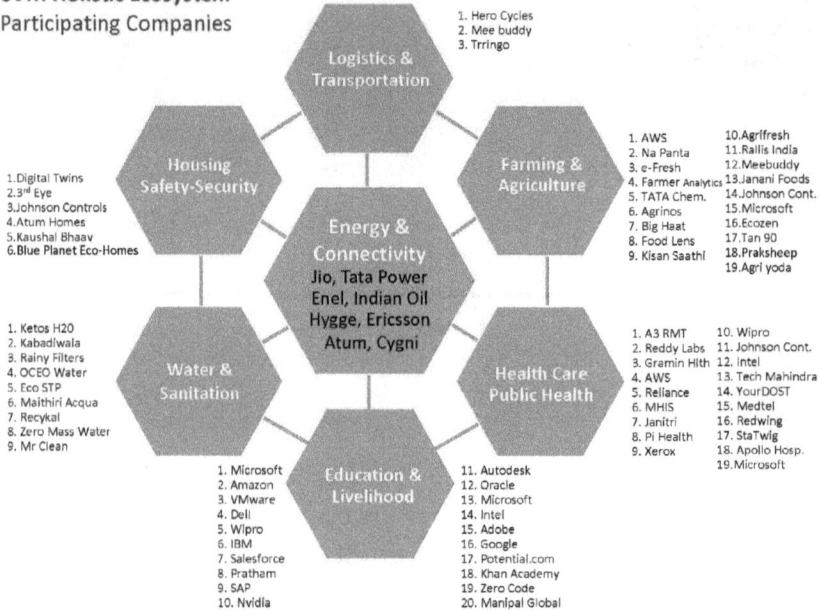

Logistics & Transportation
1. Hero Cycles
2. Mee buddy
3. Trringo

Housing Safety-Security
1. Digital Twins
2. 3rd Eye
3. Johnson Controls
4. Atum Homes
5. Kaushal Bhaav
6. Blue Planet Eco-Homes

Farming & Agriculture
1. AWS
2. Na Panta
3. e-Fresh
4. Farmer Analytics
5. TATA Chem.
6. Agrinos
7. Big Haat
8. Food Lens
9. Kisan Saathi
10. Agrifresh
11. Rallis India
12. Meebuddy
13. Janani Foods
14. Johnson Cont.
15. Microsoft
16. Ecozen
17. Tan 90
18. Praksheep
19. Agri yoda

Energy & Connectivity
Jio, Tata Power
Enel, Indian Oil
Hygge, Ericsson
Atum, Cygni

Water & Sanitation
1. Ketos H20
2. Kabadiwala
3. Rainy Filters
4. OCEO Water
5. Eco STP
6. Maithiri Acqua
7. Recykal
8. Zero Mass Water
9. Mr Clean

Health Care Public Health
1. A3 RMT
2. Reddy Labs
3. Gramin Hlth
4. AWS
5. Reliance
6. MHIS
7. Janitri
8. Pi Health
9. Xerox
10. Wipro
11. Johnson Cont.
12. Intel
13. Tech Mahindra
14. YourDOST
15. Medtel
16. Redwing
17. StaTwig
18. Apollo Hosp.
19. Microsoft

Education & Livelihood
1. Microsoft
2. Amazon
3. VMware
4. Dell
5. Wipro
6. IBM
7. Salesforce
8. Pratham
9. SAP
10. Nvidia
11. Autodesk
12. Oracle
13. Microsoft
14. Intel
15. Adobe
16. Google
17. Potential.com
18. Khan Academy
19. Zero Code
20. Manipal Global

But even with solid funding, a well-defined structure, essential technologies, and all of the other prerequisites described here in place, an ecosystem will still fail without one additional essential piece to the puzzle: the right leadership. UC Berkeley professor, David Teece describes these leaders as people with "dynamic capabilities." Like Steve Jobs and Winston Churchill, they may difficulty to get along with, but they're impossible to get along without.

Leadership with Dynamic Capabilities

OLD WAY	NEW WAY
Balance Sheet Approach	Dynamic Capabilities of HR

Balance sheet" view of assets and capabilities

Little emphasis on "orchestration" as the key success factor.

Heavy emphasis on soft assets which assist in orchestrating deployment and redeployment

Key Success Factor: Rapid deployment

Takeaway: What is essential is no longer on the balance sheet. What is essential has migrated to the capabilities of people enabled by the digital access to tools. Leaders with dynamic capabilities orchestrated by talented people win the war

Such leaders maintain laser-like focus on the task at hand to make sure it happens.We can liken their role to the human will and determination to survive the storms of life despite the obstacles that might arise. The dynamic capabilities of such leaders will be an important asset to the Rebuilding India Initiative. An effective ecosystem needs a combination of "transformers" with dynamic capabilities and skilled implementers who provide day-to-day operational expertise.

Two Types of Leadership
Leaders Make Things Happen

1. Executors: Implementation Capabilities
2. Transformers: Leaders with Dynamic Capabilities

	Managing Leaders Implementation Capabilities	Open Innovation Leaders Dynamic Capabilities
Purpose	"Do Things Right" Technical Efficiency	"Do The Right Things" Adapting / Integrating
Schemes	1. Operational 2. Administrative 3. Governance	1. Sensing 2. Seizing 3. Transforming
Imitability	Easy	Difficult

Source: Prof. David Teece 2012

One of the best-known business ecosystems was Apple's introduction of an online music store (later to include books, movies, games, and other media). The iTunes ecosystem included the devices and software marketed by Apple as well as the music marketed by established music record labels. There were various technical and business innovations that were key to making the ecosystem a success, such as the ability to buy individual songs rather than an entire album. standardization of pricing for individual songs, and copy protection for the digital music files.

Some of these had been previously tried with less success; Apple's success was largely a result of the combination of all of these elements, along with the inclusion of virtually all the major music labels so that consumers could buy into the Apple music ecosystem with the confidence that whatever music they wanted would be available.

More generally, ecosystems create scalable and sustainable economic business models by sharing risks, reducing costs by spreading the total cost across many participants, and streamlining various components of the cost structure such as supply chains and distribution channels.

An effective ecosystem – like effective partnerships – will typically exhibit the following attributes (summarized with the acronym **SMART**):

- **S**implicity, Scalability, and Sustainability
- **M**aintenance Friendly
- **A**ffordability
- **R**eliability
- **T**ime Saving

Effective ecosystems demonstrate another trait: They are minimally viable. That is, they use the least resources required to sustain themselves and their ability to create value for all participants. Unessential additions should be avoided as part of the ecosystem itself. To be clear, individual participants may find it advantageous to layer additional elements as part of how they engage in the ecosystem. But if those elements aren't an essential aspect for all participants, they shouldn't be baked into the ecosystem itself.

Maintaining a Consistent Flow of Information Through Recurring Information Exchanges

Explorations into new ideas – such as innovative business models, transformative government programs, or academic R&D exercises – may trumpet their early success, only to have that initial fanfare quickly fade away. Why do so many initiatives – drawing on the knowledge and insights of many accomplished leaders – fail to ultimately have the impact they could?

One reason stems from the short shelf life of ideas and information. Whether an idea flourishes or fails isn't simply a function of how good the idea is. It also has to be compelling enough to keep key stakeholders engaged. If an idea appears to be stagnating, funders may lose interest in supporting its continued development. The best academic researchers may find it to be a less compelling topic. Corporate support for ideas often targets the ideas that appear to have momentum and "buzz" surrounding them. Consumers tend to adopt new products that they perceive to be part of an emerging standard.

But it's often the case that to those closest to these new ideas, the merits are so obvious and so compelling that they're blinded to the need to do at least a little bit of "marketing" around them. (This is perhaps particularly true among academics and government agencies where the notion of a meritocracy – the tendency for the best ideas to naturally rise to the top – may have a built-in bias.)

With this concern in mind, the participants at our BIFI defined a mechanism to ensure that the ideas being incubated by the group would achieve an ongoing level of visibility, both internally within the group and externally to a broader audience that could provide additional input and find additional channels to apply the ideas and learnings. An advisory council will provide monthly briefings on the progress of the group to NITI Aayog, the Indian government's policy think tank focused on pursuing sustainable development among the state governments of India.

Structuring a Plan
With this framework established – thinking outside the box defined by a balance sheet mindset, striving for equitable partnerships and robust (and SMART) ecosystems, and creating and sustaining a steady communications channel – we set out to develop a

detailed tactical plan of attack. The primary focuses for this plan were to:

- Lay the groundwork for a boom in the services sector
- Develop the world's largest talent pool
- Provide basic services to the rural majority

In a moment, I'll offer a summary of some of the specific learnings that surfaced among the participants of the forum. But first I want to share a few high-level insights that emerged as common threads across several of the presentations and discussions. Despite the challenges on everybody's minds – the pandemic, the various financial disruptions exacerbated by the pandemic, uncertainty about the future – there was a generally optimistic attitude about the opportunities that lay ahead for India. There was also a surprising degree of clarity and consensus surrounding the specific challenges to be addressed if we were to make progress against our objectives.

First, there was agreement that our overarching objective – establishing India as the second manufacturing hub for diversified global supply chains – was indeed an achievable goal. (This should never be assumed.) Some of the key drivers that will play a key role in turning this goal into a reality were:

- **Emerging technologies and applications for the manufacturing sector.** Technology serves as a driver that offers a multiplier effect for accelerating many other factors as well, such as improvements in sustainability, facilitating legislation, strengthening engagement with academic institutions, and enhancing the degree of trust among stakeholders.
- **Sustainability value chains have become a critical goal in and of themselves,** in alignment with government initiatives. They are no longer viewed as a "nice to have" option, but are instead an essential element of any viable solution.

- **Engagement and partnership with leading academic institutions.** An essential path for accelerating the development of innovative solutions and the creation of knowledge can be found through close relationships with research and development initiatives in academia.
- **Facilitating the legislative and law-making process.** India's position in the global value chain also requires more robust input on and facilitation of the mechanics of government on the part of businesses, including established corporations as well as new firms aiming to expand into the Indian market.
- **Elevating trust within the global ecosystem.** The volatile dynamics of the global ecosystem – from the ongoing impact of the COVID-19 pandemic to the shifting economic dominance of geopolitical players (notably China), and the relationships between India and leading economic powers including the U.S. – complicate the challenges any one country must reckon with. But this volatility also suggests opportunities for change to take place at an unprecedented pace. A key factor determining whether the difficult challenges of today will open up the possibility of positive outcomes or will devolve into chaos lies in our ability to strengthen the degree of trust between India and other members of the global ecosystem, as well as among various stakeholder groups within India.

Another key set of conclusions addressed the need to improve and enhance digital infrastructure for learning, from early education to vocational training and skill development:

- **Government support for early education.** In rural areas especially, one of the keys to empowering educators is to ensure adequate infrastructure for reliable electricity and Internet access. Without these essential resources, it's often difficult for educators to access high-quality materials.

- **Government support for better utilization of higher education.** Many leading technology companies – including IBM, Microsoft, Adobe, Salesforce, and SAP – can envision the benefits that would result from stronger government support for higher education programs they could partner. Such partnerships could provide relevant training in technologies such as AI, machine learning, blockchain, cloud computing, and application development. This would provide targeted students and recent graduates seeking employment with high-demand skills, a boon for both employers and employees.
- **Government support for NGOs.** Similarly, stronger government support to ensure that NGOs and their funding institutions have access to relevant technological platforms would help them facilitate support for initiatives in both early and higher education.
- **Partnerships with research entities.** In addition to the value of partnerships among government, academic, and corporate stakeholders, independent research entities can drive initiatives that will benefit their business and academic counterparts.

Another group of challenges identified by the assembled group as important topics to address focused on issues related to the creation of ecosystems with the potential to mitigate the challenges and risks (many of which have been exacerbated by the pandemic):

- **Pandemic-resilient solutions are essential.** Systemic changes in the economy need to factor in the impacts of not just the COVID-19 pandemic, but of future pandemics as well. The impact of disruptions of this scale extends beyond the epidemiology of the virus, but also includes effects on the economy and on social structures that need to be addressed as part of an effective solution.

- **Robust solutions are essential.** To address the needs of both urban and rural areas, solutions must be affordable, scalable, and broadly accessible. These characteristics are interrelated and are all necessary elements for a solution to succeed; like a three-legged stool, solutions simply won't work without all of them present. Collaborative efforts, often in the form of public-private partnerships, are an essential part of the process enabling such robust solutions.

- **Education is an essential key at the individual, organizational, and ecosystem level.** While there may often be awareness of the need for vocational training for individual members of the workforce, the need to educate at the organizational level is often overlooked. But organizations as a whole need to understand new structures and processes that enable quantum leaps in progress toward ambitious goals. Even more broadly, education at the level of the ecosystem is often a necessary prerequisite for driving systemic change. For example, rural communities need to become aware of the opportunities that improvements in connectivity can offer to them to enhance their quality of life.

- **Embracing the full potential of digitalization is a critical step for enhancing quality of life.** In many areas – particularly rural areas – there is little appreciation of the multi-faceted value of digital technologies. Digital technologies can improve the quality of life in rural areas in a multitude of ways. For example, farmers can become better connected to real-time information about their markets, reducing costs and enabling them to realize better prices. Digitalization can enhance access to affordable quality healthcare, and can facilitate financial inclusiveness, closing the gap between the quality of life among those in urban and rural areas.

To spur the flow of creative thinking among the participants in this forum, we asked them to think about several questions, including the following:

- What do you think the world will be like in 2030?
- What specific plans does your company have to leverage open innovation as part of your growth strategy?
- What are the elements of your current ecosystem, and how do they help you achieve your company's objectives?
- In the vision of the future we've envisioned – in which India becomes one of the world's manufacturing hubs – how will that ecosystem need to change?
- What KPIs will you use to measure success in the emerging landscape?

A Foundation for Growth

Several of the speakers and participants in the forum highlighted more specific strategies behind their approach to growth and specific tactics they believe will help achieve the overall objective of rebuilding India. In addition, several shared their insights that provided evidence that India has the necessary resources, motivation, and spirit to achieve such an ambitious transformation.

For example, Amitabh Kant, CEO of NITI Aayog, noted the extraordinary degree of adaptability and resilience demonstrated by Indian startups throughout the response to the pandemic. Indian production of ventilators and other healthcare equipment was able to ratchet up so much that the country became a significant exporter of these goods. Indian startups with experience and expertise in telemedicine and mobile apps were able to accelerate the deployment of healthcare using contactless data-driven techniques.

Perhaps even more significant was his observation that India's development efforts have resulted in a trajectory that runs counter to global trends – in a positive way. Globally, foreign direct investment (FDI) – that is, investments made by firms and individuals in one country into business activities based in a different country – has declined (down 42% in 2020), while India's FDI continues to increase (up 13% in 2020). The government has driven policies designed to encourage FDI – removing over 1,400 rules and regulatory barriers – as part of the country's efforts to enhance opportunities to elevate those trapped by poverty and limited to low-level agricultural work.

One factor attracting global capital into India has been the country's ability to scale innovative technology. For example, there are already over a billion sets of biometric data available for appropriate identification purposes. Similarly, India has become the only nation in the world with more than a billion mobile phones, laying the foundation for the most promising infrastructure for innovation in the twenty-first century.

Building on the Baseline

Sunil Munjal, the chairman of Hero Enterprise, pegged the volume of international trade at $19 trillion annually. Of this, China accounts for over 13% of the total, with India's share at around 2%. With rising concerns over China's growth from the U.S. and other countries, many see an opportunity for India – along with other countries (including Vietnam, Indonesia, Thailand, Bangladesh, and Brazil) – to improve their global trade footprint, particularly in the manufacturing sector.

In contrast with many other countries, India's current political context places it in a favorable position to build its share of global trade. In a diverse range of sectors – including pharmaceuticals, automotive equipment, chemicals, and electronics – India is viewed as an attractive location for many global supply chains. More than 1,000 companies have already been identified as potential manufacturers for which India could become an appealing manufacturing center.

Supporting this optimistic perspective, the chairman of Hero Cycles, Pankaj Munjal, noted that countries such as Vietnam and Indonesia may have a strong presence at the moment but lack the resources, skills, and infrastructure to scale the way India ultimately will be able to. Praveer Sinha, the CEO of Tata Power, India, offered a related perspective on India's experience and advanced technological capabilities in the power sector, a crucial backbone for any industrial activity. One representative example of the maturity and sophistication of India's ability to drive continuous improvement in the power sector was a recent partnership with Lawrence Berkeley National Lab exploring development of microgrids particularly suitable for rural areas. Such microgrids may ultimately help provide electrification to the 1.2 billion people globally who have no access or limited access to electricity.

Along with infrastructure to ensure reliable access to electricity, reliable access to IT platforms and services are also an essential ingredient for rebuilding India. Dr. Malik Tatipamula, the CTO of Ericsson, noted that his company had already located a global AI center focused on 5G opportunities in India, a reflection of its belief in the country's technical prowess, and was actively involved in numerous partnerships with various research institutes and innovation centers.

Many other powerful and intriguing ideas focused on rebuilding India as the world's number two manufacturing hub. Many of them addressed five key paths to reaching this objective:

- Judiciously leveraging technology that supports all necessary aspects of the manufacturing supply and value chains.

- Maintaining a focus on sustainability, particularly in the manufacturing and energy sectors, aligning with government initiatives and goals.
- Fostering partnerships among businesses and academic institutions.
- Facilitating legislative and regulatory processes, with an eye toward creating new opportunities for both corporations with a strong foothold in the Indian market as well as new firms aiming to develop a new presence.
- Emphasizing trust across the global ecosystem, particularly in light of the impact of the pandemic as well as other geopolitical uncertainties.

Reinventing Business Models

In many cases, however, the steps for businesses seeking to participate in the expansion of India's potential as a global manufacturing hub will require more than simply extending current practices, or taking a more aggressive stance on current practices. What's needed is a process of significant reinvention of their business models.

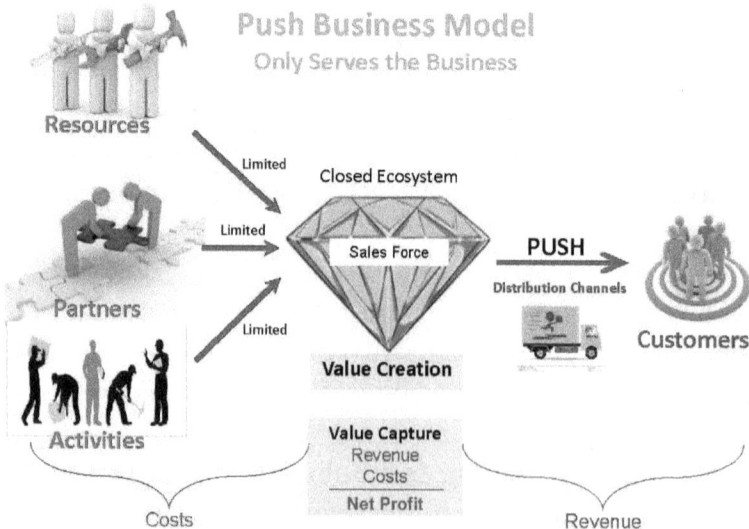

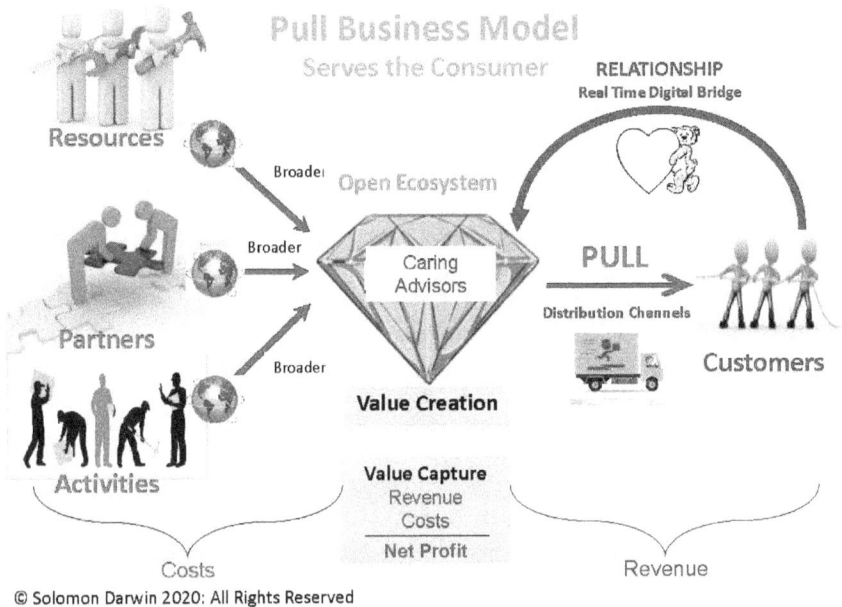

Pull Business Model
Serves the Consumer

RELATIONSHIP
Real Time Digital Bridge

Resources

Broader

Open Ecosystem

Broader

Caring Advisors

PULL

Distribution Channels

Partners

Broader

Customers

Value Creation

Value Capture
Revenue
Costs
Net Profit

Activities

Costs

Revenue

Traditional businesses operate using either push models or pull models. In the more familiar push model, decisions are driven by the business to serve its needs. In the pull model, businesses leverage open innovation to co-create outcomes with customers that serve the needs of both the business and the customers. Today's customers tastes and preferences are changing daily, and they increasingly expect products to reflect those rapidly changing wants and needs. Not only do they want to shape what they want, but they also want a say in how they'll pay for it and how and when it will be delivered. Making this work successfully requires frequent reinvention. Real-time digital communications channels between customers and businesses are essential. Businesses must also learn to capture data without inconveniencing or alienating customers, tasks where technologies such as big data and AI algorithms play a major role. As you may have guessed, our Rebuilding India Initiative is based on the concepts of the pull business model.

A critical change, as shared by Dr. Amir Homayounfard, professor of innovation and marketing strategy in the business school at the University of Essex, will be for businesses to increase their emphasis on developing and offering a more robust service ecosystem. Services, he observed, contribute a disproportionately high contribution to GDP. Some figures suggest that although only 31% of the labor force in China is engaged in services, they account for 61% of that country's GDP. Moreover, services are an essential part of a holistic offering that's attractive to businesses seeking to source their manufacturing.

In addition to rounding out the value proposition with more robust service offerings, leveraging specific emerging technologies and models of innovation are important keys to creating a stronger value proposition for manufacturing. Technologies that enable the leveraging of knowledge and information – such as AI, machine learning, automation, big data analytics, and database-driven customer relationship management (CRM) – yield crucial improvements in business outcomes. For example, despite the increasing complexity of many industries, they are able to define and manage scalable standardized objectives while simultaneously creating opportunities for personalized objectives for products and services targeting distinct market segments.

Similarly, emerging models for facilitating and propagating new ideas in R&D and commercial communities – such as open innovation – go hand in hand with the development of robust ecosystems for services. Leading global manufacturers such as Apple, Tesla, Boeing, and BMW have maintained their competitive advantage not only through improving their manufacturing value chain, but by building a complete ecosystem of services around their products. In India, the government has highlighted the practices of open innovation as a powerful strategy for smart manufacturing across many different service sectors.

The Value Proposition of Open Innovation.

Open Innovation draws on the power of: Leadership's Dynamic Capabilities, Triple Helix, Social Capital and Shared Value.

Triple Helix
· Equal Participation of Government, Academia and Business

-> Funding
-> Knowledge Creation
-> Revenue

Social Capital
· Enabling Absorbation of Information and Knowledge

· Power of Communities to Facilitate Change to Overturn Redundant Laws and Policies

Open Innvovation Framework

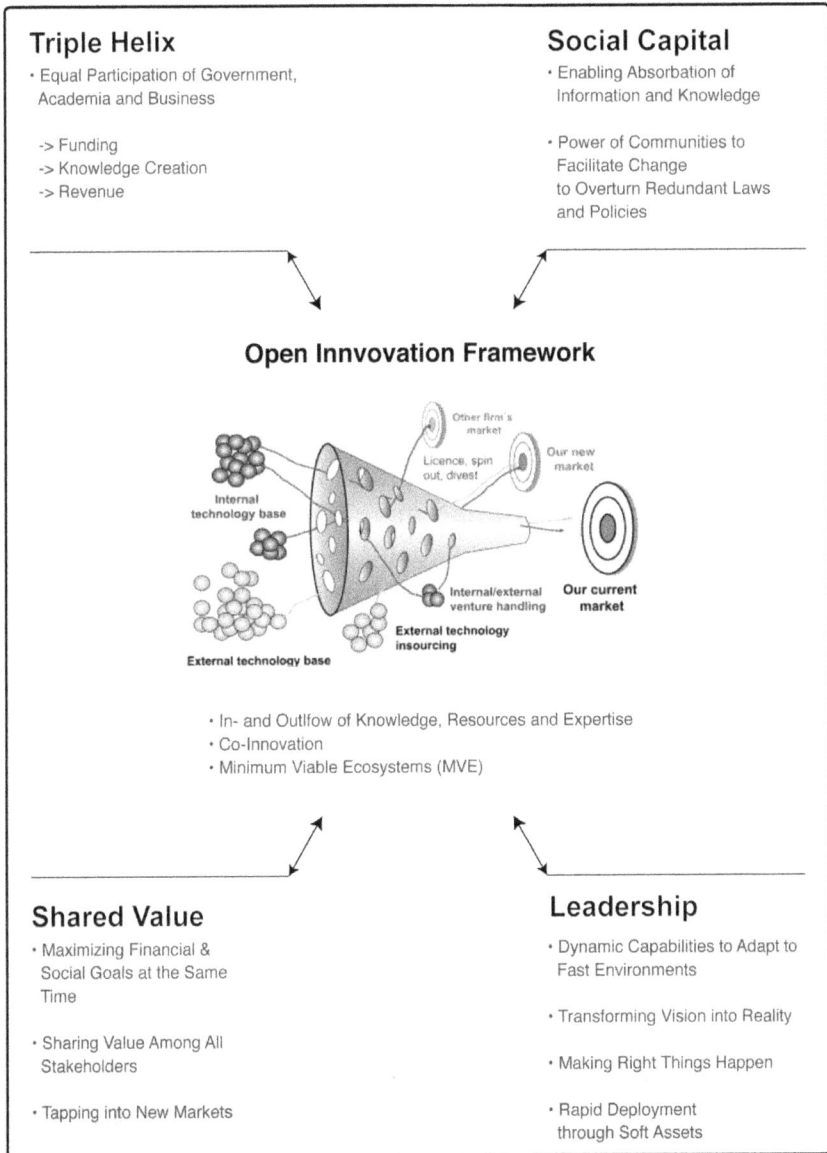

· In- and Outlfow of Knowledge, Resources and Expertise
· Co-Innovation
· Minimum Viable Ecosystems (MVE)

Shared Value
· Maximizing Financial & Social Goals at the Same Time

· Sharing Value Among All Stakeholders

· Tapping into New Markets

Leadership
· Dynamic Capabilities to Adapt to Fast Environments

· Transforming Vision into Reality

· Making Right Things Happen

· Rapid Deployment through Soft Assets

Nandan Nilekani, the co-founder and non-executive chairman of Infosys, offered an example of a government initiative, the eVidya program, that could leverage technology to propel a quantum leap in early education across the country. As part of this program, all textbooks in India could include QR codes and topic IDs that would bridge the digital and analog realms. But he also noted that technology is not the only component needed to drive this transformation, as different states would still have different approaches to assessment, content expansion, and teacher training and development. A national skills-certificate program – managed digitally – could offer a national standard as an alternative.

Indeed, the value of efforts to enhance early education could offer rapid dividends when combined with programs to facilitate entrepreneurship among young students, as outlined by Alok Ohrie, President of Dell Technologies, India. In partnership with NITI Aayog, Dell's Student Entrepreneurship Program provides students with the opportunity to spend 10-months at an alternative school where they can receive mentorship from Dell team members. Dell's Aarambh program extends the early education initiative further, training teachers and mothers to use digital devices to enhance opportunities for learning.

Other companies have established programs to help advance early learning opportunities. For example, Rahul Sharma, Present of AWS, India, noted that the AWS-Educate program was providing cloud credits at no cost to 200,000 students across India to help facilitate a generational leap in education on topics such as AI, the Internet of Things, and cloud architecture.

Transforming Ideas into Change
This collection of observations and accomplishments barely begin to scratch the surface of what was shared at this forum. And

the attendees of the forum only represent a small fraction of the activities already in motion focused on the objective of rebuilding India.

Clearly one takeaway that's hard to avoid from what was shared is the sheer volume of ideas and initiatives focused on the opportunity to expand and accelerate India's role as a global manufacturing hub. It also becomes apparent – after you've absorbed all of these concepts and analyze the common threads among them – how clearly aligned they are around a fairly small handful of common themes. Our team has found it useful to think of these themes along two axes. One axis is the group of four distinct stakeholders playing major roles in this transformation:

– Business
– Government
– Academia
– Customers

There are, of course, other ways to define the universe of stake-holders. For example, NGOs are important stakeholders playing a significant role in this shift for India, and we certainly don't mean to leave them out from this discussion. However, we believe that NGOs often wind up playing a role similar to one of these other groups. For example, some NGOs serve an analytical function similar to the role played by academia. Other NGOs often operate as customers for particular types of goods or services. And at other times, some NGOs act very much like a business. So the absence of NGOs from this list isn't meant to slight the role that they play – it's simply a reflection of the fact that, for purposes of this analysis, their impact is reflected by some combination of the other groups on the list.

The second axis in our analysis is the collection of topics and themes that kept recurring again and again. These topics focused on the needs to:

- **Speed** up the digital transformation
- Stimulate internal and external **creativity** through open innovation
- Build **ecosystems** with bridges to share risks and costs and resources
- Be **adaptable** and diversify internal transformation and mindset to adapt to the changing landscape
- **Diversify** smartly

And as you have seen, there is no shortage of ideas, pilot programs, and – in some cases – initiatives that have already successfully scaled into ongoing efforts. However, the "missing link" across these stakeholders and program domains is the much-needed foundation of trust. Without that foundation, each of these goals is met with resistance:

- Efforts to accelerate programs invariably run into speedbumps
- The most creative ideas are met with a heavy dose of skepticism
- The natural participants in new ecosystems are reluctant to join in (acting out the one-liner from Groucho Marx: "I refuse to join any club that would have me as a member")
- Adaptability gives way to sticking with tried-and-true approaches, regardless of whether they work
- Diversification is put off until "later" in favor of sticking with yesterday's winning strategies, regardless of whether they're past their prime

These counterproductive attitudes can be found among each of the stakeholder groups. But they are most pronounced when one stakeholder group finds itself dependent on a different group. That's when the absence of trusting relationships becomes most apparent, and has the most deleterious effects.

Building Blocks for a Foundation of Trust
The lack of trust has led many global corporations to take a pass on the opportunities to grow in India. When businesses contemplate making investments in India – particularly for manufacturing operations – the country compares favorably against other options when the yardsticks are economic ones. The labor pool, resources, technology base, infrastructure, government-driven incentives, and other traditional measures position India well against other countries with a similar goal of increasing their share of the global manufacturing capacity. However, when assessing the levels of trust both within the country and between Indian stakeholders and their counterparts in other countries, the perception of India falters.

You might ask: If trust is such a necessary prerequisite for a country to succeed in becoming a manufacturing partner for other countries, how has China managed to become the manufacturing hub of the world? Any objective assessment of China's relationships with other countries would surely question the degree of trust many countries have in their relationships with China.

While it may be true that many other countries don't necessarily trust China – the Chinese government, in particular – the relationship has often been a marriage of convenience in which China has willingly absorbed jobs and even entire industries that other countries don't want. This has often become an ongoing, if unhealthy relationship – one that works economically, if not so much socially or individually. India, as a democracy, can't accomplish the same things the same way. The country operates with different priorities – for example, it allows workers to strike, something that doesn't fit the Chinese paradigm.

In other words, as other countries have contemplated manufacturing partnerships in China, the terms have been so attractive that they are often willing to overlook their lack of trust. By contrast, India's value proposition is compelling, but it (along with other modern democracies) competes on a different playing field.

As mentioned earlier, a critical initial step in building trust is to engage in a dialogue with other stakeholders. And a key element of that dialogue is often missing: Asking questions to understand the needs, hopes, and fears of the other parties.

Raising these questions is important for several reasons:

- They open the door to better mutual understanding of each other
- They signal to the other party that while you may not know everything about them, you've taken the trouble to understand them well enough to ask meaningful questions
- They communicate that you value what they have to say, even when it might be something difficult for you to hear

By asking meaningful questions, you increase the level of trust that other parties will have in you. And it's also likely that the act of asking those questions will increase the degree of trust that you have in the other parties.

The goal of the process of raising these questions is only partly about understanding the answers to the questions. More crucially, the goal is to understand the communications failures and misunderstandings among the stakeholder groups.

With any kind of model involving multiple stakeholders, one of the easiest traps to fall into is a failure for each group of stakeholders to understand the others. This can be a result of different language, vocabulary, and shared references and touchstones. Or it may be an even deeper schism involving different values and priorities. Or it may stem from differing senses of urgency and appropriate timeframes. The bottom line is that these factors often result in failures of trust that hold back progress.

Even the process of producing a book such as this one can fall into traps created by lack of trust, or lack of understanding among different stakeholder groups. There's usually a built-in bias that winds up defeating the purpose of the exercise. For example, if a book is written by an academic, it's very hard for that book to avoid viewing everything through an academic lens. A different kind of book or workshop created by an experienced entrepreneur will inevitably be colored by that perspective.

This book is designed to tackle that schism. Instead of trying to provide simple answers, our goal is to offer a series of questions from each of the stakeholder perspectives. We don't have all the answers; our goal is to make you think about your own answers. Yes, we'll suggest answers to some of these questions, but we also hope you'll disagree with many of them.

QUESTIONS FOR STAKEHOLDERS

*"Trust is the lubrication that makes it possible
for organizations to work."*

– Warren Bennis

WHAT FOLLOWS ARE a series of questions on each of the five topics, *from* each of the four stakeholder groups *to* each of the three other stakeholder groups. (If you do the math, that winds up as a total of 60 lists of questions.)

Our goal for each list was to articulate questions in the same spirit that a "mystery shopper" explores a transaction for consumer packaged goods. The maker of a dish soap doesn't ask secret shoppers about the chemical formulation of the soap, or the environmental hazards of the manufacturing process, or the costs introduced in various steps of the manufacturing supply chain. What they need to uncover is that the smell of the soap makes customers think of their grandma's house, or that the packaging is off-putting because it reminds them of negative memories.

So, for example, we want to help the Indian government understand how customers really feel, what foreign businesses contemplating an investment in India need to know, and how academics can play a more vigorous role in achieving the government's objectives.

Wherever possible, we've provided links to resources that may provide background about the issue raised by the questions, or context that elaborates in more detail about why we feel the question is an important one.

For each of the five topics, there will be:

Customer questions and concerns for:

- Academia
- Government
- Industry

Academia questions and concerns for:

- – Customers
- – Government
- – Industry

Government questions and concerns for:

- – Customers
- – Industry
- – Academia

Industry questions and concerns for:

- – Customers
- – Government
- – Academia

You'll likely note that many of the questions are broad "Can?" and "How can?" questions, rather than more specific "Who, what, when, and where?" questions, or more philosophical "Why?" questions. Our goal has been to identify questions that can spark conversation and much-needed debate, not provide answers to straightforward factual matters. Even if the answer to a "Can?" question ("Can the government provide this particular improvement that would benefit business?") is a disappointing "No...", it can still advance the dialogue and can improve understanding, particularly if it explains the reasons behind the answer ("No, because the law would first need to be changed") Similarly, we aimed to avoid "Why?" questions that could easily meander into interesting – but not necessarily productive – armchair philosophy.

One final note before diving into the battery of questions: Any list of questions such as this is certain to spark ideas for:

- Additional questions
- What you think the answers are
- Who you think would be uniquely qualified to answer a particular question

SPEED

MOVING QUICKLY IS always an essential part of any competitive endeavor. But when it comes to the race to gain market share as a manufacturing hub for the world economy, speed is especially crucial. That's because many of the key battles for market share as a global manufacturing partner will be won or lost as a result of which countries are best ready, willing, and able to facilitate the digital transformation of various elements of the manufacturing value chain.

Customer questions for industry

What kinds of questions do customers have for their counterparts in industry? The nature of their questions will vary depending on many variables:

- *What type of customers they are (large business accounts, individual consumers, repeat customers, one-time customers, and so forth)?*
- *What kinds of businesses they're dealing with (products, services, commodities, custom-made goods, makers of large goods that need to be stored or transported long distances, producers of small items made locally, etc.)?*
- *What are their most pressing concerns (quality, quantity, speed of delivery.)?*

For many customers, the logistics surrounding transportation are a primary concern. In their ideal world, truck bodies would be standardized (with a similar containerization approach to the model that transformed shipping). This would streamline loading and unloading, offer greater flexibility and more options for shippers, and increase operational efficiencies in general. Standardization of pallet sizes would facilitate faster turnaround times and standardize warehouse designs, simply by creating a common standard to be used across logistics facilities at airports, on riverboats, and at other facilities including seaports, inland container depots, container freight stations, multi-modal logistics hubs, and warehousing clusters.

Another topic on the minds of many customers is finding reassurance that, should the need arise, they'll be able to receive a prompt refund. This isn't simply a matter of customers who'd like the option of returning purchases; it's often crops up when a transaction fails. A refund can involve an exchange of information between three or four parties, each of which has their own mechanisms for processing the refund. Many of these processes – including those that live within the banking ecosystem – require manual oversight. The upshot is that a customer may find themselves short of funds for something they were never able to actually purchase for as long as five to ten days.

Q.1 How can you speed up the launch of products that solve real problems for customers? Products and services need to offer convenient and practical solutions to the functions your customers are trying to accomplish, which often change rapidly. Slow product development means that customer needs may change before a solution even becomes available.

Q.2 How can you speed up logistics so that products and services reach customers on time?[1]

Q.3 One deterrent to online transactions are the delays (often 5-10 days) involved in issuing refunds not just for returns but also for failed or cancelled transactions. How can this process of refunding the customer's money be sped up to encourage more people to buy online?[2]

Q.4 Customers also need to be better informed about the value of investing in services such as educational blogs and instructional knowledge base content. How can providers of such services do a better job of educating potential customers about their value and about how to use them?

Q.5 How can you create new research and development (R&D) processes to develop new products and services, and improve and accelerate existing processes to deliver a better return on investment with more user-centric results? Total R&D expenditure in India was just over one tenth of one percent of net sales in FY 2019 – higher than in previous years, but a much smaller percentage than other major global powers.[3]

Customer questions for government

India's Consumer Protection Act of 1986 mandates that all cases must be settled within 90 to 150 days. But as of July of 2019, there were 18,518 pending cases in various distinct consumer courts (and another 3,549 cases at the state level). When the backlog in delivering justice via the legal system gets longer and longer, it can make you skeptical about whether there really is any justice.

Likewise, there are many business practices that routinely involve lengthy delays and inefficiencies. For example, warehousing in India is a highly fragmented industry, with most warehouses having an area of less than 10,000 square feet, and 90% of all warehousing lack the benefits of mechanized or unionized operations. This translates into more time needed to get basic tasks done, and higher levels of inventory losses. While the government isn't directly responsible for these inefficiencies, many feel that the government has failed to play a leadership role in modernizing and standardizing essential parts of the manufacturing supply chain such as warehousing and transportation.

Q.1 How can you speed up the process of the grievance redressal system run by the government of India and fast-track trials in consumer courts?[4]

Q.2 How can you speed up logistics processes (for example, with dedicated rail and air transport) to provide quicker delivery of products and services?[5]

Q.3 How can you expedite and improve government-funded facilities such as warehouses and cold-chain/freezer storage and transportation of products so that products reach the customer safely

73

and intact? At present, 90% of this sector is unorganized (that is, operated by unlicensed and unregistered vendors).[6]

Q.4 How can the government better scrutinize middleman operations to provide more effectively and quickly mitigate abuses by monopoly businesses?

Customer questions for academia

Many customers are acutely – and personally – aware of the R&D gap between India and other countries. Or at least they're aware of the ramifications of this gap. India's investment in R&D continues to hover in the range of 0.6-0.7% of GDP, far lower than comparable investments in other companies with many similar characteristics, such as South Korea, Israel, and Japan. Indeed, in 2019 India was ranked 52nd (out of a total of 129 countries) on the Global Innovation Index.

This R&D gap translates into a lower rate of training for those entering the workforce, less on-the-job training to help the workforce stay current on new innovations, and gaps in the talent pool available to businesses.

Q.1 Despite the fact that they have received formal training, 33% of trained youth remains unemployed largely due to lack of appropriate skills. How can academia provide more job-focused learning and skill development?[7]

Q.2 Can educational institutions speed up R&D to create better goods and services despite low budgets for R&D?[8]

Q.3 Can academic research accelerate the process of improving customer knowledge about different industries, products, and services, as well as about customer rights?

Q.4 How can academia focus their research to equip consumers and businesses with better technology that enhances the buying experience?

Industry questions for government

First, the good news: In a relatively short period of time, India jumped 79 spots (from number 142 to number 63) in the World Bank's ranking of countries that are easiest to do business in. The biggest challenges where India still lags, however, are in parameters such as the ease of starting a business, a category in which India sits near the bottom (number 136) in 2019.

Another area in which many industries would like to see the Indian government take more initiative are actions to bolster the country's savings and investment rates. Particularly given recent business disruptions – driven by the pandemic and other factors – many feel the government should be more vigorously considering new policies that would lead to tax reform.

Q.1 How can the government update industrial and mercantile law so that new businesses can ramp up more quickly?[9]

Q.2 Can the government speed up trial courts to remove the bottlenecks they currently create for businesses?

Q.3 Can the government speed up tax reforms for industries?[10]

Q.4 Can the government help to drive faster movement of goods and services, such as with new infrastructure like dedicated freight and air corridors?[11]

Industry questions for academia

Many in the business community believe that academia can play a stronger role in helping to close not just the R&D gap but to boost GDP as well. With $9.4 trillion in goods and services produced in 2017, India is the fourth-largest economy in the world. But China, the European Union, and the United States all have GDPs of twice that amount.

By focusing on key areas for research, new models for innovation, and training that will better prepare graduates to excel in the workplace, some see potential for academia to help steer industry toward a more vibrant path to progress on these fronts. Such efforts may also help to bring down unemployment levels, which have been as high as 40% for freshly trained graduates.

Q.1 Can academic institutions better support R&D initiatives into new technologies, goods, and services – more quickly and with less friction?[12]

Q.2 Can academia help foster skill development for personal growth in the workforce with targeted and focused training and workshops?[13]

Q.3 How can academic institutions support R&D efforts to achieve sustainability goals such as reducing industrial pollution?

Industry questions for customers

Understanding what customers want is always a vital part of business planning. In particular, businesses can help speed up the cycle of creating, marketing, and selling new products by finding more effective ways to develop that understanding and to reap the benefits of a customer base that appreciates their latest offerings.

Q.1 What can industry do to better motivate customers to spread positive word of mouth?

Q.2 How can industry streamline feedback processes to get better input from customers about their experiences with products and services?[14]

Q.3 What steps can industry take to interest customers in the new concepts behind many new products and services?

Government questions for customers

With no national blueprint for the infrastructure of logistics and standards, there's little uniformity in these arenas across India. These inconsistencies show up in everything from commerce to the legal system. This often results in uncertainty for customers, which hampers their ability and willingness to explore new ideas, new products, and new business models. Ultimately, this also drives costs up. Similarly, the overwhelming majority – around 90% – of the warehousing and cold-chain logistics industry is unorganized, so it doesn't benefit from any kind of union-mandated standards or practices.

While there can be benefits in favoring local autonomy over nationalized approaches, there are also missed opportunities resulting from operating outside of international standards – particularly for things like logistics management. Obtaining a better understanding of customer preferences and priorities is an important step for the government to accelerate adoption of new products and services.

Q.1 How would you prioritize the government's efforts to improve, increase, and standardize infrastructure for fast movement of goods and services so that products can reach customers sooner?

Q.2 How important is it to you for the government to invest in systems designed to upgrade warehousing and cold-chain facilities to reduce damage or spoiling in the journey to the customer?[15]

Q.3 What steps would you like to see the government take to engage customers in providing suggestions and advice on services and products they receive on a more timely basis?

Q.4 Is it a priority to speed up the process of the grievance redressal system? What steps do you think the government should prioritize?[16,17]

Government questions for industry

A starting point for driving policy improvements is for the government to ensure that it has a clear understanding of the hopes, fears, and priorities in the business community. While these could turn out to be a jumble of contradictions, it's often the case that there are commonly held viewpoints that simply need to be more clearly surfaced. And of course the simple action of eliciting input and feedback will help to build trust, even when stakeholders may not wind up with the outcomes that are most desirable for them.

Q.1 In what specific ways would you like to see the government improve transportation logistics to speed up the movement of goods and services?[18]

Q.2 What tax reforms do you feel would help industry in the near future?[19]

Q.3 What policy changes do you feel would help expedite the approval of new businesses?

Q.4 What changes would you advocate to help reduce the backlog for and delays in many court trials?[20]

Government questions for academia

Given the country's low level of investment in R&D, low ranking on the Global Innovation Index, and high levels of unemployment for both long-time workers and freshly trained graduates, the government can benefit from the involvement of the academic community in identifying new approaches to accelerate innovation and economic changes that will speed up the process of rebuilding India.

Q.1 What new models for structuring government-sponsored financial assistance to academia would bolster R&D in the short-term future?[21]

Q.2 What would be needed for academia to accelerate R&D into ideas for government policies that would generate more benefits for industry?

Q.3 How might academia quickly develop and deliver training programs and workshops to enhance skill development for ongoing growth among the government workforce?[22]

Q.4 Could academia offer any research to help provide better technology for specific government functions?

Academia questions for government

Academics – basically by definition – flourish when there is more information available. Government operatives often follow almost the opposite approach, keeping much information cloistered or on a need-to-know basis. Some of the most valuable questions for academics will simply be to gain a better understanding of the current baseline for government policies, operations, and objectives.

Q.1 Is there a government roadmap to provide financial assistance to encourage more rapid and focused R&D?[23]

Q.2 What is the government's roadmap to help academia speed up research to support better technology for government functions?

Q.3 What R&D priorities would most help the government accelerate the creation of better business policies to foster the rebuilding of India?

Academia questions for customers

India's overall economy lags behind other countries with which it's economy is frequently compared. Not only is investment in R&D low and unemployment high, but India's GDP per capita, inflation, tariff rates, and corporate tax rates show poor performance when compared not just with China, but with Canada, Germany, Indonesia, Israel, Japan, the UK, and the U.S.. To help reverse these trends, academia needs help from customers for a wide range of goods and services to better understand what kind of R&D, training programs, and innovative technologies should be prioritized.

Q.1 How can academia provide quick learning (including skill development) to those who provide goods and services to customers, particularly given the high unemployment rates that often stem from the lack of appropriate skills?[24]

Q.2 How should educational institutions prioritize R&D spending to help streamline the creation of better goods and services, delivering the best ROI for that investment in R&D?[25]

Q.3 Is academic research a helpful avenue to help improve customer knowledge about industries, products, services, and consumer rights?

Q.4 What academic research topics could help facilitate better technology that would streamline the buying experience which would, as a result, stimulate the economy?

Academia questions for industry

Academia and business have a long tradition of working closely together. But that doesn't necessarily mean they understand each other. While academics may have an excellent understanding of the big picture or the theoretical underpinnings of the marketplace, they may not always appreciate what factors have the most practical impact on a day to day basis. Proactively seeking concrete answers on specific topics would help accelerate some of the transformations necessary in the process of rebuilding India.

Q.1 What academic research would be most useful to support your question for the development of new products, services, technologies, and business models and practices?[26]

Q.2 Can academia provide more, and more focused, expedited training and workshops for skill development to support the personal growth of the workforce?[27]

Q.3 What R&D programs would most help industry pursue sustainable development objectives, such as reducing pollution?

CREATIVITY

THERE ARE A few different strategies for achieving a quantum leap forward in your progress toward an ambitious objective such as rebuilding India. One approach could be characterized as the brute force strategy. If you can throw unlimited resources against a problem, there's a good chance that – despite a number of impediments and setbacks – you'll eventually succeed. Some might characterize China's economic leaps forward in the second half of the twentieth century in this way.

But when resources are more limited – either because they don't exist, or because a society's values impose limitations such as how harshly one is willing to treat its workforce, for example – a different strategy is needed. Innovation and creativity can drive the same kind of quantum leaps, when effectively harnessed.

In particular, open innovation is a particularly effective approach to not merely driving creative change, but driving it at a rapid pace. By facilitating the sharing of ideas across all participants, the opportunity for each company or research institute to piece together all the necessary elements to create something new, open innovation benefits not just each individual team but the overall ecosystem – India as a country, in this case – as a whole.

And for open innovation to succeed, one of the prerequisites is a heightened degree of trust. And for that trust to flourish, robust dialogue among all the stakeholders is an essential first step.

Customer questions for industry

Businesses often put enormous thought and effort into everything they do – every decision they make about new products, choices about how to invest in streamlining sales and support functions, and balancing the tradeoffs (between, say, keeping prices low vs. adding new functionality) that are necessary in the marketplace.

This process may seem self-evident to those running the business. But to their customers, these outcomes may be mystifying. Customers may be quick to assume that, in fact, there's been no thought to a complex set of tradeoffs. And even though a business may have agonized over a particular decision, it may not have been an informed choice.

There are many opportunities for the business community to develop more creative channels that enable customers to weigh in with their ideas and perspectives. And that process starts with opening a dialogue and asking questions.

Q.1 What prevents you from launching more products that address real problems in a more convenient manner?

Q.2 Many startups are flourishing, but overall R&D remains very low compared with many other countries. Can Indian businesses produce more innovative products and services?[28]

Q.3 Do you have a blueprint to create channels that leverage customer ideas for and perspectives on the innovations needed in the marketplace?[29]

Customer questions for government

In 2016, India ranked 25th on the World Bank's LPI index that pegs countries based on their performance with logistics. This was a significant step up from India's 2014 ranking – 54th – reflecting a variety of improvements. But it still inidicated it still indicated various deficiencies in the country's logistics infrastructure, a lack of integration among stakeholders, a deficit in skilled manpower, and comparatively slow adoption of new technology. This performance suggests a number of questions for government that customers would like to raise and understand.

Q.1 How can you leverage innovative methods for efficient logistical facilities (such as dedicated rail and air transport) to facilitate faster delivery of products and services?[30]

Q.2 How can you facilitate better government-funded warehouse, freezer, and cold chain facilities for proper storage of products to ensure reliable delivery of undamaged goods?[31]

Q.3 How can the government reduce the monopolistic control that some firms have over middlemen and traders?

Q.4 How can the government leverage new innovations to mitigate corruption and malpractice related to customers' rights?

Customer questions for academia

Just as customers perceive government as needing an infusion of creativity, they likely have similar questions for academia. But their questions for academics focus less on logistics and legalities and more on innovations in products, services, and processes.

Q.1 Can academia help deliver new techniques for the workforce to develop new skills that will enable the production of innovative, less expensive, or more timely goods and services for customers?

Q.2 How can academia help streamline the process of researching, selecting, and purchasing products and services in a faster and easier way?

Q.3 Customers benefit from the broader adoption of open innovation techniques, although this approach can run counter to the mindset of secrecy and siloed information that typically characterizes traditional corporate research labs. How can academia promote swifter adoption of open innovation practices?[32]

Government questions for customers

There are many topics about which customers lack any detailed knowledge, or may even have inaccurate biases that they're unaware of. For example, in a recent ranking of the Global Innovation Index, India was ranked 57th. Many people will find this surprising, believing that India is a leader in the information technology revolution and must surely rank much higher. While India does indeed have good credentials in many areas, the country's overall performance adds up to a less competitive position than many might expect.

On the flip side, there are innovations that could drive a substantial boost to the economy far more easily and more quickly than many might think. For example, logistics amount to 14% of India's total GDP, substantially higher than the amount spent by the U.S., Japan, and Germany (which range between 8.5% and 11%). But many believe India's expenditures could be brought down to that range and that the country's exports could be boosted by as much as 8% solely as a result of making improvements in the "last mile" portion of the transportation network.

By raising the right questions for customers, the government can create an opportunity to educate customers on both facts and opportunities they may be unaware of.

Q.1 What new ideas would you suggest for new policies to defend consumer rights?

Q.2 What suggestions do you have for the government to incorporate innovative ideas to provide infrastructure for the fast movement of goods and services so that products reach the customer on time?[33]

Q.3 What steps would you like to see the government take to accelerate innovations in the market so that new and improved products reach the customer (including goods exported to other countries)?[34]

Q.4 What steps can the government take to include customers early in the development process of policies related to open innovation?[35]

Government questions for industry

Taken as a whole and compared with other nations, Indian industry suffers from a number of somewhat basic deficiencies. For example, many companies in India have no way to analyze their basic plant layouts, are often stymied by fundamental tasks such as long-term planning, and lack any meaningful innovation strategy or plan for staffing innovation initiatives.

Some of the roadblocks that industry faces stem from broad societal challenges, such as digital illiteracy, antiquated infrastructure such as nonexistent (or slow and sporadic) internet access – that fall under the purview of government more so than business. Other issues – such as issues pertaining to taxation – arise as a result of the lack of coordination across various departments and functions. To achieve the goal of rebuilding India, the government needs to expand its palette of creative solutions to the problems that wind up holding back the private sector. An important first step toward finding creative solutions is to engage in a more robust dialogue between government and industry.

Q.1 How would you like to see the government prioritize financial assistance for investment in innovative ideas to accelerate the creation and delivery of products and services?[36]

Q.2 What steps can government take to align different market forces to expedite the creation of new and improved products and services?

Q.3 How can the government help industry launch or accelerate digital transformation initiatives?[37]

Q.4 How can the government help industry leverage open innovation and other innovation ecosystems?

Government questions for academia

If we're honest, neither government nor academia has the best reputation for creativity. But perhaps all that's missing is fostering a more open environment between these two institutions in which new ideas can emerge, one characterized by trust rather than by guarded skepticism. Some basic questions could open the door to more fruitful dialogue involving these two stakeholder groups.

Q.1 How would you prioritize financial assistance for R&D related to open innovation and other approaches that could provide a quantum leap forward in innovation for products and services?[38]

Q.2 What is the overall roadmap for R&D in academia on topics that could spur open innovation?

Q.3 How can academia help industry and other stakeholders deploy innovations in the market so that more new and improved products and services are created – and more quickly?

Q.4 As open innovation becomes a factor in a wide range of R&D domains, its impact should be analyzed through a variety of lenses: For individual corporations, at the inter-organizational level, at the intra-organizational level, from an extra-organizational perspective, and at industrial, regional, and societal levels. How can academia help with this complex analysis?[39]

Academia questions for customers

The 2015 India Skills Report revealed the depth and some of the details of the skills deficit in the Indian workforce. Among students applying for roles in the workforce, only about a third had the skills required by the jobs they were applying for. This gap is also reflected in a number of business practices. For example, Indian entrepreneurs tend to focus more (compared with the countries it typically competes against) on business model innovation than on new products and services. And while Indian consumers demonstrate a high degree of digital savvy, Indian business demonstrates a relatively low level of adoption for various technologies driving digital transformation in the economies of other countries.

Q.1 As we explore innovative ways to help facilitate skill development, what particular new skills would help you the most in advancing your own career?[40]

Q.2 In recent times, innovation in India tends to focus on business models more so than development of new products. Should we reverse that emphasis?[41]

Q.3 Digital transformation is an urgent goal for many businesses. What kinds of innovation in digital transformation do you think would result in the most meaningful benefits for you?[42]

Academia questions for government

One of the prerequisites for an environment that sparks creativity is having a clear and comprehensive snapshot of all of the variables that might come into play. But investing in understanding the economy and the marketplace hasn't been a priority for stakeholders in India. For example, according to the 2014 ESOMAR Global Market Research Report, over $40 billion was spent globally on market research that year. The Asia-Pacific region invested only 15% ($6 billion) of this total, and India accounted for just over 4% ($252 million) of the Asia-Pacific total – or just over half a percent of the global total. Clearly more and better data will be essential to inform India's innovation roadmap.

Q.1 What is the government's roadmap to support academia to carry out more research on innovation?[43]

Q.2 What is the government's roadmap to expand and enhance market research to better understand and identify opportunities for innovation that would support the rebuilding of India?[44]

Q.3 How can the government incorporate open innovation to streamline cost-effective R&D in the future?

Q.4 How can the government facilitate opportunities for academia to develop essential training and workshops for different groups of stakeholders?

Academia questions for industry

Given the high levels of unemployment – stemming from a lack of critical skills for the workforce, even among new graduates – there are obvious benefits to be had from closer dialogue between the academic and business communities. Clearly there should be stronger alignment on the specific skills that have become necessary for new graduates to have acquired prior to entering the workforce. But there are also opportunities for some creative thinking about new models such as open innovation for cultivating innovation and high-growth industries such as Bollywood and other entertainment realms.

Q.1 What priorities would you recommend that academic institutions focus on to support research that would enhance industry's R&D efforts?[45]

Q.2 What kind of training and workshops could academia develop that would enhance workplace skills that leverage the potential of open innovation?[46]

Q.3 The output of Bollywood now exceeds that of Hollywood. What role can academic institutions play in identifying comparable opportunities for growth markets?[47]

Industry questions for customers

As mentioned earlier, industry would benefit from beefing up its investment in market research about what customers want and how they would prioritize various tradeoffs in the products and services they need, bringing that investment closer to the norm for comparable economies. In addition, the opportunity to better understand customers could be improved by exploring not just specific market research questions, but also by exploring different approaches and channels for holding that dialogue with consumers. In other words, industry doesn't just need a better understanding of the questions that market research can answer, but businesses could also benefit by raising some "meta" questions about how best to go about the process of conducting market research.

Q.1 If you could allocate R&D budgets into the new types of products and services you'd most like to purchase, where would you be most likely to invest?[48]

Q.2 What mechanisms for providing feedback and input on products and services would you be most willing to use (to help steer our development of innovative products)?[49]

Q.3 What factors capture your attention about new products in the marketplace?

Industry questions for government

India has made significant improvements in the country's position on the World Bank's competitive ranking of the counties of the world, jumping up 79 notches to rank 63rd for ease of doing business. But this represents a jump from a very poor competitive standing to merely a mediocre one. And on other measures – such as ease of starting a business – the country continues to hold a low competitive ranking. Clearly there are many avenues in which other countries have achieved better results or achieved them more quickly. This suggests a number of questions that industry will want to raise with government.

Q.1 Industrial and mercantile law can impede and stifle business innovation. Can the government update the most egregious of these laws to remove or reduce barriers to innovation?[50]

Q.2 Logistics are also often an impediment to creativity in business. Can the government help facilitate faster transportation capabilities, dedicated freight corridors, and other measures that would help industry adopt new and creative solutions for the movement of goods and services?[51]

Q.3 What kind of input can industry provide to help government create effective policy for the adoption of open innovation?

Industry questions for academia

What does industry consider to be the function of academia, at least when it comes to the economy? Certainly educating a steady stream of graduates who will be equipped with the right skills to enter the workforce is a key objective. Conducting R&D into key technologies and other new innovations is another. And exploring new approaches and methodologies for the R&D process itself – such as open innovation – is another.

Q.1 How can academic institutions support industry with R&D that helps to drive the development and adoption of creative new technologies and other innovations?[52]

Q.2 What is academia's roadmap for quickly improving training and creating workshops to better equip the next generation of workers?[53]

Q.3 How can academic programs help broaden support for and understanding of open innovation in industry?

ADAPTABILITY

THROUGHOUT ITS HISTORY, India has proven to be extremely adaptable, again and again. The country has reinvented its economy, its political systems, and its social structures. One recent example: In the early phases of the COVID-19 pandemic, Indian startups were able to shift gears to address the shortage of medical equipment such as ventilators to such an extent that the country became – almost overnight – an exporter of such equipment.

But when it comes to a number of basic approaches to its economy, India has been reluctant – or unable – to implement changes as rapidly as other global economies. Whether you attribute this to a deeply rooted history of traditionalism, to stubbornness, or to other social and cultural factors, the net result is that India has fallen behind many other countries on several key measures that are essential for India to become the world's second manufacturing hub.

There's no reason to believe that India won't be able to once again adapt to be successful in achieving this objective. The first step is for each of the major stakeholder groups to develop trust with one another, by engaging in vigorous dialogue to surface greater awareness of the need for adaptability and new ideas about how to make change happen more easily and more quickly.

Customer questions for industry

While some businesses and some sectors of industry have embraced a variety of digital technologies, there are large swaths of the economy that have yet to embrace some of the most fundamental digital technologies. Only 34% of India's micro, small, and medium enterprises (MSME) have embraced technologies such as software-as-a-service solutions for interacting with employees, customers, and suppliers. And a mere 7% (in a 2019 survey) have fully adopted such technologies. While half of the respondents were aware of the potential benefits, the vast majority lacked the knowledge, skills, or budget to implement digital solutions.

Q.1 How can industries more fully embrace new and improved technologies to increase production and reduce costs so that innovative and more affordable products reach customers?[54]

Q.2 How can industries develop faster modes of transportation for goods and service so that products reach customers on a more reliable and more timely basis?

Q.3 What is your blueprint to create channels for capturing customer ideas and perspectives that would facilitate your transformation toward more robust use of technology and product diversification – and, as a result, greater customer satisfaction?

Customer questions for government

One of the most common points at which customers bear the brunt of government policies that have fallen behind the policies of more competitive countries is transportation infrastructure. For those using shipping services, the lack of standardization of truck bodies pallet sizes, and loading docks leads to inefficiencies, delays, and high costs. Standardization of warehouse designs continues to lag, as does integration of trucking with other modes of transportation.

Road congestion also results in delays and low productivity. For example, the average productivity for a truck in India is about 200 km/day, a figure that could be increased to 350-400 if congestion was reduced. India also has a very low capacity of modern warehousing facilities.

Beyond transportation and related logistics issues, IT capacity also lags substantially behind competing countries. These infrastructure deficits suggest a number of the questions about adapting to the constantly evolving needs of the economy that customers would like to raise to government leaders.

Q.1 How can you adapt India's infrastructure to embrace innovative methods for new and efficient logistical facilities (such as standardization, dedicated rail and air transport, and integration across all transportation modes) to provide faster and less expensive delivery of products and services?[55]

Q.2 How can you adapt guidelines for warehousing to encourage new methods of storing products so that products reach customers without damage or spoilage?[56]

Q.3 As individual businesses undergo their own internal transformations, how will you develop policies that factor in these diverse changes?

Q.4 Increased competition has widened the choices available to customers for goods and services. This ratchets up customer expectations which, in turns, sometimes leads companies to attempt to attract customers in underhanded ways. What is the government's plan to maintain a market that is both free and fair?

Customer questions for academia

In the 2019 Periodic Labour Force Survey (PLFS), the unemployment rate among urban 15-29-year-olds (a very large population) was nearly 24%. It's possible that this high level of joblessness stems largely from one of the major drivers of unemployment among the population as a whole: the lack of suitable formal or informal training.

And not only do many lack the necessary training to become effective members of the workforce, many also lack the necessary training to become effective and efficient consumers. For example, low awareness of widespread counterfeiting (coupled with inadequate enforcement) have led to a boom in counterfeiting, according to a report from the Federation of Indian Chambers of Commerce & Industry, a non-governmental trade association.

Another apparent blindspot is the low level of investment in R&D. While some sectors (notably automobiles and pharmaceuticals) have ramped up R&D spending a bit, India lags behind most of the countries with which its economy is frequently compared.

Ultimately, consumers bear the burden of all of these knowledge gaps. These are complex challenges, unlikely to be solved by one group of stakeholders acting on its own. But they're all challenges that have been addressed – with varying degrees of success – in other countries. This suggests a number of questions that consumers may want to suggest as topics for academia to investigate.

Q.1 What kind of skill development training would help new graduates adapt to the changing needs of the employment market?[57]

Q.2 In a fast-moving market for many types of goods and services, what kind of academic research would help streamline how customers can find and purchase the best products for their needs?

Q.3 How can academic research help customers better understand how to protect their own interests and their rights as consumers?[58]

Q.4 How can academic research help industry speed up R&D that would drive faster and better targeted innovation of goods and services, particularly given the relatively low level of investment in R&D?[59]

Industry questions for customers

Compared with its frequent competitors, India underinvests in formal research initiatives such as market research and R&D that might provide insights into the needs, concerns, and priorities for customers. Reversing this trend is likely part of any strategy to significantly increase India's share of the world's manufacturing capacity.

But in the near term, industry can bolster its understanding of the consumer mindset by engaging in more dialogue. Such dialogue serves multiple purposes. For industry, it surfaces new data points and helps to identify specific topics where more detailed or more formal research will be needed. And for consumers, it provides some reassurance that industry is aware of and interested in them.

Q.1 Describe some of the ways in which your life is changing, and how that might translate into changes in the goods and services that you need the most?[60]

Q.2 What are your expectations from industry regarding your experience as a customer? In particular, what processes work best for you in sharing your input and feedback on our products, unmet needs, and mechanisms for providing feedback?[61]

Q.3 What steps can industry take to help customers understand new concepts that don't yet exist, to better align R&D efforts with the unmet needs of our current and potential customers?

Industry questions for government

For industry to adapt to dramatically and rapidly changing circumstances – whether it's pandemic or geopolitical dynamics – it needs as much flexibility as possible. Yet it often finds its hands tied. Sometimes that's a result of inertia and maintaining its own status quo. But often it's the result of factors driven by other stakeholders, such as state and national government entities.

For example, India's logistics capabilities suffer from a lack of standardization that in many other countries is driven by the government. India lacks a policy framework for effectively driving or reforming standardization in transportation, warehousing, and other matters of logistics. At the same time, tax policies have discouraged corporate actors from consolidation that would drive standardization from the corporate side of things.

Q.1 How can the government adapt policies that shape industrial and mercantile law so that new business with fresh ideas for the rapidly changing market can get established more quickly?[62]

Q.2 How can the government help industry adopt techniques such as standardization or the creation of dedicated air or freight corridors that would promote faster movement of goods and services?[63]

Q.3 How can industry help the government create policy or financial incentives that would promote the adoption of new technology in a fast-changing environment?

Industry questions for academia

The primary advantage that startups have over large, established compa-nies is that they can readily change. They can learn from mistakes, they can respond to changing circumstances, they can pivot to a new business model once it becomes clear that the previous idea just isn't working. This ability to constantly adapt can be enough to overcome a host of disadvantages: Lack of experience, lack of resources, lack of respect from or standing in the world.

In contrast, for large companies, the tables are turned. They have resources and respect, they have experience to draw upon, and they have prominent standing among their colleagues. Their brands have name recognition. But what they often lack is any degree of flexibility that would allow them to adapt to a changing world as quickly as startups can.

One can find elements of both the startup and the venerable behemoth in India's history. The country is enormous, its territory is sprawling, its his-tory is vast. And yet, the country has also reinvented itself countless times – the most recent reinvention having begun less than a single lifespan ago.

The task of rebuilding India hinges on the country's ability to act (at least in certain ways) more like a young country – a startup. The trick is to also retain its strengths as an ancient and venerable world power (at least in certain ways). Juggling these two personas – the lumbering giant and the nimble newcomer – is a delicate balance about which industry would be wise to seek counsel from academia.

Q.1 How can academic institutions support industry's efforts to become more nimble? What areas should we focus our R&D efforts on to reflect today's changing landscape?[64]

Q.2 Can academic institutions explore ways for industry to become more adaptable in the changing landscape for India and the country's economic objectives?[65]

Q.3 What kind of research can academic institutions offer that would help industry produce more goods and services to keep pace with customer demand?[66]

Q.4 What type of R&D can academia provide to help industry minimize its environmental impact?[67]

Government questions for customers

As the economy and environment change at an ever-increasing pace, the government needs to be more agile in developing policies related to customers. "Customers" includes the buyers in business-to-business industries as well as small and micro businesses, along with individual consumers of products and services. The priorities for each of these groups may differ, but all would like to see government policies that are more responsive to their needs.

An essential first step for government to create more responsive policies is for it to engage in more dialogue with all levels of consumers to better understand their needs and the dynamics that are driving continuous change.

Q.1   In today's environment, customers need faster delivery of goods and services. What ideas do you think would enhance the country's infrastructure for rapid and reliable movement of goods and services?[68]

Q.2 What ideas would you like to see implemented in policies that defend consumer rights?

Q.3 What innovations for warehousing and storing products would you like to see implemented to reduce damage and spoilage of merchandise throughout the delivery chain?[69]

Q.4 What steps would you like to see government take to include customers earlier in the development of policies that encourage economic transformation?

Government questions for industry

In an economy in which small and micro businesses play such a major role, MSMEs often find themselves in a "fish out of water" situation. The fabric of much of the country's infrastructure often leaves them in a precarious situation when it comes to access to such business necessities as electricity, Internet access, transportation, and warehousing. And they're often excluded from the infrastructure behind an even more fundamental resource: Money.

MSMEs often find themselves to be excluded from the financial system, or at least find themselves forced to overcome a number of hurdles that their big business counterparts rarely have to deal with. They may not have credit extended to them, or it may take so long that it becomes impractical. They often suffer from "information asymmetry," with banks and other financial institutions having access to far more information than they do. They may find it difficult to meet expectations and norms regarding collateral.

Government has made certain efforts to adapt to these economic realities. For example, on the recommendation of the Prime Minister's Task Force Committee, the Bombay Stock Exchange launched an SME Platform, which lists MSMEs and could pave the way for a new source of finance that attracts investors from diverse fields. What other initiatives would industry like to see to help the government adapt to current and future economic realities?

Q.1 How can the government provide technological assistance to industries so that they can work more effectively and efficiently?

Q.2 What form of financial assistance to small businesses would most help them keep up with the changing environment?[70]

Q.3 What mechanisms for sharing feedback and suggestions to the government work best for you?

Q.4 What is industry's roadmap for dealing with future uncertainties and changing business requirements?[71]

Government questions for academia

Understanding the challenge of adaptation – why some businesses or entire countries are better at it than others – is a task better suited to academics than to government officials. Before government policies can be crafted to steer the country in the right direction, the government should equip itself with a more robust understanding of the nature of adaptation itself: How does it happen? What leads it to stall out? What government actions lead to the kind of alignment across all stakeholders that will be needed to successfully rebuild India as a manufacturing hub for the world?

Q.1 Does the academic community have (or can it develop) a road-map for understanding how countries can successfully adapt in a rapidly changing and increasingly diversified environment?

Q.2 How can the government most effectively provide financial assistance to academia for conducting research and development related to adaptability?[72]

Q.3 How can academia provide research to identify the most appropriate technology for government functions?

Q.4 How can the government help academia provide the technical training necessary for different stakeholders in relation to changing technology?[73]

Academia questions for customers

It's one thing for the academic community to understand the statistics that challenge India's workforce, such as the severe skills gap (only about a third of employees have skills that match employer expectations, according to the 2015 India Skills Report). It's another matter entirely to understand the root causes that need to be addressed.

Similarly, academics may be able to quantify the digital divide separating the haves and the have-nots when it comes to online access. But do they understand the full picture driving the digital gap?

Academia has no shortage of data to factor into their analysis – for example, the median age of India's population is 28, with half of the population younger than 25. But this fact may be hard to reconcile with the skills gap in the workforce or the digital divide among the population. More dialogue between academia and customers will be useful in helping both groups understand how they can more vigorously adapt to the changes at play in the country.

Q.1 What is the most effective way to provide you with better skill development?[74]

Q.2 What kind of research on digital transformation would be most useful to you?[75]

Q.3 How can academia help customers better understand and use new technologies and techniques that would help you manage today's changing business environments?

Q.4 What kind of R&D would you find most useful?[76]

Academia questions for industry

Both academia and industry often strive to understand trends that affect large groups of people. For example, both groups should be concerned that of the 688 million Indians falling within the working-age category, many are jobless because they lack the skills that employers need them to have.

Industry, however, also tends to focus on finding solutions that can work for one individual at a time. A training program that helps one person secure a new job is a success – at least if it can be scaled to work for many individuals. By engaging in more dialogue, academia and industry can often find partnerships that tap into each group's strengths – academia providing insights on the broad, societal impact of an initiative or new approach and industry figuring out the tactical details of one-on-one deployment.

Q.1 How can academic institutions provide support for industry R&D to surface new ideas for creating or improving goods and services that meet the needs of rapidly changing business environments?

Q.2 How can academia help to develop training and workshops to help workers and new graduates develop the right skills for today's workforce?[77]

Q.3 Smart training processes are key to retaining employees, improving employee engagement, and filling missing skill sets within an organization. How can academia help industry with these goals?

Q.4 With the rise of new digital solutions for every aspect of business and personal life, cybercrime and security risks are on the rise. How can academia help to mitigate these challenges?[78]

Academia questions for government

Which is harder: Planning for the future, or learning from the past? Both can be daunting – particularly if they're done separately. Too often, the academic community focuses mostly on trying to understand where we've been while the government is tasked with thinking about where we're headed.

More dialogue between the two communities will help inform both groups – especially when it comes to wrestling with questions about how to adapt with constant change.

Q.1 How can we help government be more vigilant in dealing with issues such as risk and compliance?

Q.2 How can academia help the government identify laws, policies, procedures, and legislation that are overdue for reform?

Q.3 What is the government's roadmap for providing financial assistance to academia to carry out more research?[79]

Q.4 How can academia help the government plan for future societal disruptions and uncertainties?

ECOSYSTEM

THE ESSENCE OF an ecosystem is similar to the timeless question about the folly of reinventing the wheel. We might all eventually stumble across the value of using a round shape as a device to make things easier to move, but it would take a lot longer than just saying, "Oh, I should just put wheels on this thing."

Likewise, an ecosystem provides a mechanism that anybody can use to share risks, costs, and resources. In a sense, an ecosystem is an agreement that everyone will standardize on the same choices of certain aspects of goods or services. While there will still be plenty of room for competition, an ecosystem focuses the competitive differences on particular aspects of the product. For example, Apple's ecosystem for digital music defines various technical and business parameters, which enables record labels and musicians to focus their attention on competing to produce the best musical offerings.

The upshot of the introduction of ecosystems is much like the impact of having national and global standards. When the width of railroad tracks are standardized and the size and shape of shipping containers are uniform, it greatly streamlines and accelerates international logistics and accelerates market growth. Likewise, ecosystems can streamline and accelerate everything from marketplaces to business processes to government programs.

Customer questions for government

In 2019, India ranked 68th in the Global Competitiveness Index, the World Economic Forum's global empirical assessment of a country's institutions, infrastructure, adoption of technology, macroeconomic stability, product markets, labor markets, financial systems, market size, health, skills, business dynamism and innovation capability. In contrast, China ranked 34th.

This provides an indication of the degree of dramatic change that India needs to undergo to achieve the goal of becoming the world's second manufacturing hub. The leverage provided by dynamic ecosystems can help drive this change – and quickly – but only if there is vigorous buy-in among all the stakeholder groups.

Q.1 How can the government form policies to help industries in different sectors work together to enhance production and reduce waste to reduce prices for customers?[80]

Q.2 How can government provide infrastructure for shared warehouse facilities so that multiple industries can benefit from the same modernized facilities that provide reliable and cost-effective storage services?[81]

Q.3 How can the government provide shared logistical facilities to provide reliable, fast, and less expensive transportation for products and services?[82]

Customer questions for industry

Businesses are accustomed to promoting themselves to customers on an individual basis. Even though they may have thought through the value proposition of an ecosystem that they've championed, they may not have thought about how to communicate that value – or even whether to communicate that value – to their customers.

If industry has kept to themselves about the ecosystems they're cultivating, this may prompt several questions on the part of their customers.

Q.1 How are you leveraging emerging technologies to optimize new ecosystems to share resources and reduce product pricing?

Q.2 How does your ecosystem address the logistics issues (such as transportation and warehousing) that push prices up, cause delays, and hold back progress in many industries?[83]

Q.3 What does this ecosystem do to help businesses share risk with others, and how exactly does that benefit customers?

Customer questions for academia

The academic community can also help customers understand the value and benefits of industrial ecosystems. Academia can also offer a more independent perspective, one that is less likely to sound like, for example, a justification for companies attempting to exploit customers by operating in conjunction with one another.

Q.1 Business ecosystems typically focus on supply chains, value chains, production processes, and other business systems. While there may be room for improvement in those areas, there's an urgent need to improve the skill gap in the workplace. Nearly half (48%) of Indian employers report difficulties filling job vacancies due to the talent shortfall. Even in one of the strongest sectors of the Indian economy – information technology – many skilled technician roles go unfilled for lack of qualified candidates. Are there ways that a business ecosystem can address the skill gap in the workplace?[84]

Q.2 Can customers become integral members of new ecosystems that, for example, offer innovative ways to buy products in a faster and easier way?

Q.3 Given the ongoing low levels of overall R&D in India, can educational institutions prioritize R&D topics related to creating ecosystems in which resources are shared to provide better goods and services to customers?[85]

Industry questions for customers

Even when customers don't have a formal role to play in a new ecosystem, that doesn't mean their input should be ignored or discounted. By including customers in a dialogue about their ecosystems, businesses can tap into fresh ideas, dispel fears on the part of customers, and generate enthusiasm for the new approach.

Q.1 What new technologies would you like to see leveraged in new ecosystems, and what technologies do you feel would have a negative impact?

Q.2 How important are shipping logistics – such as how long fulfilment and delivery take or the risks of damage and spoilage en route – in your perception of the value of a new business ecosystem?[86]

Q.3 What other aspects of your interaction with businesses do you think present appropriate opportunities for multiple companies to pool resources and share risks?

Industry questions for government

Constructing an ecosystem can be a powerful strategy for the companies participating and taking advantage of it. It can be even more powerful with the participation and blessings of the government. With government participation, more companies are likely to feel supportive of and comfortable with the ecosystem and will choose to take part in it. Government may also have the opportunity to align its own programs in directions that will be consistent with the ecosystem.

Q.1 Can government bring change in industrial and mercantile law that will align with ecosystems designed to help businesses share risks, costs, and resources?[87]

Q.2 How can the government provide financial help to industry to build and ramp up effective ecosystems?

Q.3 How can industry help the government create policy that accelerates the use of new technology that helps the development, operation, and ongoing evolution of ecosystems?

Solomon Darwin with Yashraj Bhardwaj

Industry questions for academia

Although there are numerous examples of successful ecosystems in industry, the concept is still relatively new and under-leveraged in the corporate community. Sometimes the simple fact of being "new in town" carries a stigma in the business community; if something was really a good idea, wouldn't it be more popular?

On the other hand, new ideas can sometimes get more of a "fair trial" in academia, where being new and different is more often seen as a potential advantage. Getting the academic perspective on questions related to business ecosystems could provide valuable guidance to industry.

Q.1 What are the most crucial elements of successful business ecosystems?[88]

Q.2 Are there particular skills that will be required to successfully implement business ecosystems?[89]

Q.3 What can you envision for advanced manufacturing facilities that could be shared by different companies – or even different industries – to streamline production, reduce costs, or enable new capabilities?

Q.4 Are ecosystems that would include both large global companies alongside MSME (micro, small, and medium enterprise) companies practical and, if so, how do you expect them to differ from other ecosystems?[90]

Academia questions for customers

Business ecosystems are launched and driven by industry, but they often directly involve customers. So they have to offer an appealing value proposition to customers as well. They may solve specific pain points for those customers, or offer them improvements. At the very least, they should avoid introducing anything negative that takes away from the value proposition of whatever the ecosystem is displacing.

And it's important to remember that to the consumer, perceptions often influence behavior as much as reality. An ecosystem that introduces elements that customers dislike, fear, or distrust – even if these concerns are completely unfounded – will face an uphill battle. Building trust among customers is a necessary step toward driving acceptance, and creating dialogue is a necessary step for building trust.

Q.1 Do you have any reservations about the notion of businesses collaborating together for the mutual benefit of all the participants as well as their customers?

Q.2 What customer benefits do you think a business ecosystem can deliver?

Q.3 Can you point to examples of a successful ecosystem that has made a positive change in the way you interact with businesses, purchase goods or services, or enhanced the logistical aspects of the interaction?

Academia questions for industry

The nature of academic research is often quite different from the way a business tends to analyze the same proposition. Academics frequently study a wide range of variables, whereas businesses tend to quickly zero in on a few familiar variables (reducing costs or increasing revenues and profits). Academics often investigate hypothetical scenarios in some unspecified future timeframe, while businesses generally focus on likely next steps.

When it comes to understanding business ecosystems, dialogue between academia and industry provides an opportunity for these two distinct mindsets to compare notes. The questions that academics bring to the business community can serve either to inform and educate their own research and thinking – or to prompt new avenues for business analysts to consider.

Q.1 What elements of potential ecosystems would help boost innovation in products and services?[91]

Q.2 Can the development of business ecosystems help close the skills gap, such as by creating shared training programs?

Q.3 Could advanced manufacturing facilities effectively be shared by multiple companies in different industries, thereby reducing the cost, accelerating production, or improving the quality of finished goods?

Q.4 MSME (micro, small, and medium enterprise) businesses are often at a disadvantage compared with large companies. They lack access to adequate and timely banking and financial services, they often have significant knowledge gaps, there may not be technology available that's suitable for companies of their scale, and they often lack the resources for basic tasks including production, marketing, modernization, expansion, hiring labor with specific skills, and resolving government snafus. Given these differences, can large companies work effectively with MSME businesses within the same business ecosystem?

Academia questions for government

Given the potential of business ecosystems to dramatically accelerate prog-ress toward the goal of rebuilding India, government may want to do what it can to facilitate their advancement. Such involvement could be helpful, or it could backfire by creating confusion as to whether the ecosystem is a business-driven initiative that will succeed or fail based on corporate objec-tives or a government-driven program that is subject to change any time there's a shift in the political winds. Academia may be able to help provide guidance to government officials seeking clarity in defining the optimal role for government in such ecosystems.

Q.1 What do you consider to be an appropriate role for govern-ment in the creation of ecosystems designed to reduce costs and risks among businesses?[92]

Q.2 Can the government frame policies to help academic insti-tutions facilitate the creation and management of business ecosystems?

Q.3 How can academia help the government design policies for industries to work together for their mutual benefit in being more productive and reducing risks?

Q.4 How can academic institutions in different regions help to design frameworks for small scale businesses to work with large companies within the same business ecosystem?[93]

Government questions for customers

Ecosystems are designed to solve a variety of problems faced by many businesses and their customers. When it comes to manufacturing, some of the most widespread challenges are the lack of reliable and inexpensive power, access to skilled and productive labor, intellectual property protection, and transportation and logistics services.

Q.1 What policies would you like to see prioritized to help update India's manufacturing capabilities through the use of ecosystems? [94]

Q.2 How important is it to you for businesses to not merely reduce costs but to also reduce wasted resources in the manufacturing process?

Q.3 Would you like to see the formation of watchdog organizations to observe how businesses work together to share risks and benefits and provide feedback to the government to inform its policy-making process?

Q.4 What mechanisms for participating in events and surveys conducted by government organizations would be most effective for you?[95]

Government questions for industry

In addition to the goals of reducing costs and increasing productivity in manufacturing, ecosystems also have the potential to reduce pollution and other forms of environmental damage. Upgraded manufacturing facilities, shared by multiple businesses, could offer an alternative to the common practices of simply dumping wastes, including toxic and hazardous materials, into open spaces and nearby water sources.

Q.1 How can businesses work together to build enhanced infrastructure that will facilitate the ability to share resources that enable them to reduce costs and increase productivity?

Q.2 How can businesses reduce pollution and other environmental damage by working together with other businesses for the welfare of the whole ecosystem?[96]

Q.3 Can businesses collaborate on R&D and protect the interests of small businesses so that small businesses and small-scale ecosystems are protected?[97]

Government questions for academia

The skills gap is affecting both large companies and small businesses. According to the 2015 India Skills Report, only a third of all students applying for positions had the skills needed for the jobs they were applying for. And among MSMEs, only 34% have embraced digital tools for communications tasks. Perhaps academia could help government explore ways that business ecosystems could work together to close this skills gap.

Q.1 Does the presence of a business ecosystem change the priority of R&D topics that businesses should focus on to improve products and services?

Q.2 Can academia provide training and skill-development programs to better equip the workforce within an ecosystem with an eye toward reducing costs and increasing efficiency?[98]

Q.3 How can academia help the government develop policy to help companies work together to reduce business risks and increase productivity?

Q.4 Can educational institutions in different regions help to create a framework for small scale businesses to work with large industries in the same ecosystems?[99]

DIVERSIFY SMARTLY

GIVEN THE RAPIDLY changing circumstances driving the economy – from the pandemic to sweeping geopolitical changes – the need for diversification has never been more urgent. Companies (and countries) that focus all their efforts on a single market can find themselves doing well, until the demand for their particular goods or services dries up.

But diversification simply for the sake of hedging one's bets across different markets can also be problematic. So-called "SMART" diversification emphasizes each of the following characteristics that comprise the SMART acronym:

S: Simplicity, Scalability and Sustainability

M: Maintenance-friendly

A: Adaptability

R: Reliability

T: Time Saving

Customer questions for industry

Customers generally appreciate having more options available to them. So when companies diversify the range of goods and services they produce and market, that's a good outcome for customers, right?

Well, not necessarily. If the business isn't diversifying in a smart (or SMART) way, they could actually be spreading themselves too thin. Can they support a broader product line with maintenance and after-sale support? In their race to diversify, have they cut some corners in the design or manufacturing stages that will leave the customer with an unreliable product?

As customers discover new and diverse product offerings, they will likely have some questions for the businesses producing them.

Q.1 Can industry create diversified products and services that solve real problems for its customers?

Q.2 What will it take for you to increase investment in R&D to drive product strategies that will bring a more diverse range of products and services to market?[100]

Q.3 What is your blueprint to create channels to capture customer ideas and perspectives for a more diverse array of products and services along with the logistics needed to deliver them quickly and reliably?[101]

Customer questions for government

India's infrastructure, logistics, and supply chains have long been riddled with inefficiencies and corrupt practices. These problems ultimately push up prices and push down productivity. And government policies and tax structures sometimes entrench these long-standing practices. Can the process of diversification also shake up some of these unhealthy habits?

Q.1 What types of policies for regulating industries would encourage more diversity of more goods at more affordable prices?[102]

Q.2 Can you develop policies that will encourage greater diversity with an eye toward reducing wasting resources?

Q.3 How can customers participate in government programs to develop skills related to diversification of products and services?

Customer questions for academia

A recent survey found that 48% of Indian employers reported difficulties filling job vacancies due to talent shortages. Even in the IT sector, one of the brightest spots in India's overall economy, many positions go unfilled due to an ongoing skills gap. As businesses diversify, this gap could be exacerbated. On the other hand, part of the SMART diversification philosophy could help workers scale their skills to close the gap.

Q.1 Can academia provide recommendations for skill-development training that provides the much-needed diversification of the capabilities of the workforce?[103]

Q.2 How can academia help industry learn how to accelerate awareness of knowledge of more diversified products and services?

Q.3 What kind of R&D can academia conduct to identify the best directions for diversification, given current limitations on investment in R&D?[104]

Q.4 Can academia identify low-cost products that industry should pursue as part of its diversification initiatives?

Solomon Darwin with Yashraj Bhardwaj

Industry questions for customers

SMART diversification will often be driven by the supply side of things – for example, looking for ways to reduce costs by amortizing manufacturing costs across multiple product offerings rather than allocated to a single product. But even when driven by supply-side considerations, it will benefit by also considering the view from the demand side of things – that is, the customer point of view.

Q.1 As industry aims to diversify, what specific products and services are you most interested in?

Q.2 What channels for providing ideas and perspectives about ongoing diversification would be most useful and convenient for you?[105]

Q.3 How important do you feel a more diversified logistics infrastructure would be for you, assuming it could provide more options, more flexibility, and better reliability?[106]

134

Industry questions for government

For many businesses, the prospect of diversification can be daunting when they're preoccupied with the day-to-day struggle for survival. To the extent that government can mitigate these challenges – whether they are related to the pandemic or to issues that predated COVID – this will better enable them to explore new paths to diversification.

Q.1 What kind of financial help can the government provide to MSMEs to allow them to focus on SMART diversification?[107]

Q.2 How can industry steer the government toward policy for adopting new technology that would help enable diversification of production?

Q.3 What changes in industrial and mercantile law can be implemented that would promote new approaches to diversification?[108]

Q.4 Can government help industries collaborate in ways that would promote more robust diversification for all parties?

Industry questions for academia

Many businesses are adept at expanding into new areas that are adjacent to the markets in which they have extensive experience. A company making one type of baked goods might expand by adding additional baked goods to their product lineup. But SMART diversification might steer companies toward areas that fall outside their comfort zone – from baked goods to the manufacture of some entirely different product that is able to leverage some of the same equipment for precision heating and cooling.

A classic example of this kind of repurposing of existing assets was the U.S. telecommunications company Sprint, which began as a railroad operation. Eventually, it discovered that the rights-of-way it controlled for its railroad tracks had more value as the backbone for a telecommunications network. Academics may be able to help provide this kind of broader view of the diversification opportunities for industry.

Q.1 What guidance can academia offer to steer industry in creative new directions for diversification?[109]

Q.2 Can academia provide guidance on advanced manufacturing technologies and techniques to help guide industry in the process of identifying and prioritizing diversification targets?[110]

Q.3 What research-driven insights can academia offer to recommend how diversification efforts can be aligned with efficient use of raw materials, infrastructure, and other resources?

Government questions for customers

The government perspective on diversification needs to take into account the goal of mitigating the ongoing impact of the pandemic and of any major business disruptions that may occur in the future. There are many quantitative indicators that can help government understand the impact on industry – revenues, employment levels, skill gaps, and so forth. But understanding how diversification can help customers is a less clearly defined challenge. Increased dialogue between government and customers can help paint a more meaningful picture.

Q.1 How can the government help customers from different regions provide their input on how government can leverage tools such as creating new policy to encourage diversification?[111]

Q.2 Is there interest in creating groups that would collaborate with government entities to change how new product offerings and services could better reflect and serve the diversification of our population?

Q.3 How can government effectively engage with customers to help them understand the potential of SMART diversification and what it can offer to consumers?

Q.4 Can customers provide input that could help government enhance the ability of industry to diversify by reducing risk and increasing production?[112]

Government questions for industry

The current set of laws and regulations regarding anti-competitive and monopolistic practices in India is fairly young. So it's to be expected that industry may adopt a cautious attitude regarding diversification into new markets. By the same token, this suggests that industry should welcome more dialogue with government to help it better understand this new framework.

Q.1 How can the government help industries collaborate and develop and manage diversified resources and services to optimize and create revenue?

Q.2 When it comes to identifying new avenues to create broader product offerings and new means of production, what are industry's R&D priorities?[113]

Q.3 How can government work with industries to formulate policies and frameworks to use resources and services across different industries to boost productivity, efficiency, and access to raw materials and infrastructure?

Q.4 How can the government provide financial assistance to MSMEs to help them pursue SMART diversification?[114]

Government questions for academia

Given high unemployment rates and an all-too-often wide gap between the skills employers need and the skills that new graduates bring with them, will diversification exacerbate these challenges? Government can attempt to preempt such issues by engaging with academia as a partner to identify new skills that will be needed as industry diversifies.

Q.1 How can academia help the government identify additional skills that will be needed as businesses strive to diversify their offerings?

Q.2 How can educational institutions provide skill training to workers to better equip them for the employment opportunities created by diversification?[115]

Q.3 Can academia collaborate with government to create a policy framework that encourages and incentivizes more diverse product and service offerings?

Q.4 What financial assistance mechanisms would you like to see government pursue to fund academic R&D related to SMART diversification?[116]

Academia questions for customers

In exploring ways to help better equip the workforce with skills needed in an increasingly diversified economy, academic institutions first need to make sure they have a thorough understanding of the workforce. Otherwise, they may find that their recommendations for training initiatives are a mis-match for the target audience they're aiming to help.

Q.1   How can academia provide the right programs for skill development that will be needed in an increasingly diversified marketplace?[117]

Q.2   Can academia develop recommendations to help accelerate and expand the delivery of relevant information and insights to customers about an increasingly diversified universe of products?[118]

Q.3 What are customer priorities for new products and services that might become available at lower prices based on the adoption of SMART diversification techniques?

Academia questions for industry

Even after a business or an industry is convinced of the benefits of SMART diversification, they may still find their efforts stalled by a dizzying array of new alternatives to consider. Not only is the number of choices more than they may be accustomed to analyzing, but they may also find themselves exploring unknown (to them) terrain. Academia can help them find a path forward by prompting them with questions to help them navigate these options.

Q.1 As you consider options for diversification, what gaps in your knowledge of potential new products, services, and manufacturing technologies would be most useful to bridge?[119]

Q.2 What financial mechanisms to support relevant R&D in SMART diversification are you open to?

Q.3 Which technologies that support advanced approaches to manufacturing – including the Internet of Things, AI, and machine learning – are you prioritizing in your approach to SMART diversification?[120]

Academia questions for government

The academic community has an opportunity to help accelerate the process of diversification in industry, by helping other stakeholders – including government entities – better understand the landscape and different options that could be pursued. To make this input as useful as possible, academia first needs to understand the existing context for SMART diversification – the needs, priorities, and existing programs that the government is pursuing.

Q.1 What gaps in the path toward SMART diversification is government aware of?

Q.2 What kinds of training programs does government feel will be necessary to equip workers in the more diversified workplace of tomorrow?[121]

Q.3 How can academia collaborate with government in the creation of a policy framework that encourages SMART diversification?

THE QUEST FOR THE JEWEL

THE HISTORY OF modern India has followed a dramatic arc. After centuries of growth as a relatively isolated country, the country had developed a thriving and diverse economy and intellectual prowess in science and the arts. The culture was permeated by a deep sense of spirituality, and there was no reason to suspect that India's continued success and prominence faced any significant roadblocks.

When the country became a British colony in 1858, it was regarded as the "jewel in the crown" of the British Empire. From an economic perspective, the reach of that empire offered yet more avenues for growth and prosperity.

For a variety of geopolitical and socio-economic reasons, Britain's global dominance reversed its trajectory in the 19th and 20th centuries. And by the middle of the 20th century, India was again an independent nation. In the ensuing decades, the global economy was shaken by a series of rapid shifts – from the emergence of China as an economic powerhouse to the explosion of the personal computers, the Internet, and other forces of digital transformation.

In business, entrenched global corporations were now regularly challenged – and often dethroned – by scrappy startups. Governments were increasingly shaped as much by social media as by more traditional lobbyists and think tanks. Academic institutions began to abandon their old traditions of remaining isolated from business and government in favor of developing complementary partnerships with those institutions.

India has successfully ridden many of these trends. But it has fallen short with others. And, perhaps most significantly, even when the country has achieved success, it has watched as other countries have found strategies that have greatly outpaced India in their growth.

Notably, China has usurped India's dominance as the manufacturing hub for much of the rest of the world. The factors driving this shift are many, and have been well documented elsewhere. However, there is one underlying factor that has been largely overlooked or downplayed, and that is the widespread lack of trust across different stakeholder groups within India. These groups include government agencies, businesses, the academic community, and consumers of goods and services. These four groups comprise what I call the quadruple helix underlying a dynamic and thriving economy. (This idea is a modification of the triple helix model developed by Henry Etzkowitz and Loet Leydesdorff.)

The previous edition of this book explored the facts behind that lack of trust among different stakeholder groups. One of the key issues that edition addressed was the unasked questions that each of those stakeholder groups had for the other groups on a wide variety of topics. Rather than attempt to single-handedly answer a comprehensive catalog of questions, that book was intended as a prompt, to encourage dialogue among the stakeholder groups. Indeed, part of the message that I hoped readers would come away with was that the simple act of asking questions to others and having those questions acknowledged could often be more important than whatever the answers might be.

That's not to suggest that the answers are irrelevant or unimportant. However, meaningful answers to this very broad array of topics should come from people with an equally broad array of perspectives and expertise. To capture those perspectives, my plan was to launch an ambitious series of dialogues with dozens of government and business leaders, along with individuals representing consumers. (With my team of partners at UC Berkeley, I felt we could reasonably represent the perspective from academia.)

We were fortunate to be able to hold a series of dialogues during a Berkeley Innovation Forum (BIF) in 2022. These took the form of group discussions and individual interviews, providing hours of first-person expert insights from the world's leading experts on the challenge of rebuilding India's economy. This was essentially equivalent to a graduate-level seminar on the topic.

Based on those insights, this book aims to move beyond a compendium of questions about rebuilding India and provide readers with an action plan they can immediately implement – as business leaders, as government officials, as academics, or as consumers in the Indian economy. The steps in the plans presented here are a synthesis of the wisdom we captured at the BIF.

Across every industry, the disruptions caused by the COVID pandemic have prompted business to rethink every aspect of what had previously been standard operating procedures or entrenched status quo assumptions. Many businesses found their entire sector had been put on pause – travel and entertainment, dining out, any healthcare services that were suddenly deemed non-urgent. And if a business wasn't directly morphed by the pandemic, most were dramatically shaken by everything from disruptions in their supply chain to having to rethink how to hold meetings remotely.

Given this degree of transformation, businesses were forced to question everything. Did they need to change their product offerings? Was their company still a viable proposition? Should they lay off staff? Cut wages? Assist remote employees working in expensive cities like New York and London to work remotely from less expensive regions?

It was, in other words, a complete reset. No options were left unexplored. Some of these resets took place practically overnight, with schools embracing Zoom and TV becoming a premium distribution channel for movies given the shuttering of cinemas. Other changes will take years to play out. And, as of this writing, it remains to be seen what will happen as the pandemic eventually winds down – or whether it will simply remain a permanent factor in our lives. Will the status quo revert to pre-pandemic norms, or will the economy continue to embrace the opportunity to question everything and continue to reset itself?

To be sure, the COVID-19 pandemic has been different – both quantitatively and qualitatively – from earlier pandemics, especially for India. The 1918-1920 Spanish Flu pandemic infected roughly a third of the world's population, and had more casualties in India than anywhere else, resulting in the deaths of at least 5% of the country's population.

COVID-19 has not only resulted in its own tragic statistics, but it is also having several fundamentally different types of impacts on today's globally interconnected world. For starters, global transportation today is far more fluid than it was in 1918, making it far easier for infectious diseases to travel across borders. And the global economy is far more dependent on global supply chains spread across the planet. Disruptions thousands of miles away can have substantial consequences on regions that may not be viral hotspots.

As a result, our strategies for coping with the pandemics of today need to embrace a different mindset, one that is open to resetting every aspect of even the most deeply entrenched business models and standard operating procedures.

And as much of an economic disruption as the pandemic has been, it is far from the only disruption currently shaking the global economy. In recent years, several forces have emerged as megatrends that – had there not been a pandemic – would be on everybody's radar as factors creating both threats and opportunities in practically every sector of the economy. A podcast series called "Hidden Forces" (https://hiddenforces.io/) that I've found to be insightful has featured episodes on a variety of topics reflecting some of these trends that, in their own ways, are resetting the global economy as profoundly as the pandemic. These include:

- The "mission economy," a notion championed by Mariana Mazzucato, a professor in the economics of innovation and public value at University College London. Her work champions the idea of a "moonshot economy" that rethinks the way we rise to meet challenges in the interest of the public good. This often entails rethinking the role of government tools and culture, and a process that emphasizes collaboration among stakeholders.
- Aside from the all-too familiar COVID-19 pandemic, society has been suffering from the impact of a different kind of pandemic – a pandemic of loneliness. So says thought leader, broadcaster, and academic Noreena Hertz in her book *The Lonely Century*. Paradoxically, a leading cause of this ubiquitous loneliness is our digital technology that many assumed would create stronger person-to-person and culture-to-culture bonds. And a major consequence of this loneliness is the loss of trust as individuals all into a vicious cycle of self-imposed isolation.
- Is income inequality an unintended consequence of modern monetary policy – or is it, in fact, a direct result of decades' worth of policy? Economic policy expert Karen Petrou suggests the latter. Inequality, she argues, may not

be the objective, but it flows directly from the way the Fed analyzes data and the way that financial markets analyze the Fed. The US economy by itself has an outsized impact on the global economy, but the patterns Petrou outlines also suggest some opportunities for other countries to gain an advantage by taking more aggressive steps to close the inequality that the US will have difficulty with because of these entrenched systemic pitfalls.

– Anyone who keeps up with the news will have a hard time disagreeing with Nicole Perlroth's belief that the cyber-arms race is heating up – and quickly. An award-winning cybersecurity journalist for *The New York Times*, she is also a regular lecturer at the Stanford Graduate School of Business. The cyber-arms race is different from other battlefronts in that it lacks all of the familiar characteristics with which we've defined conflicts for centuries: national borders, rules of engagement, and the like. And because nearly all of us (individuals, businesses, and governments) use the same systems, more or less, the challenge for a cyber-criminal who seeks to attack on multiple fronts simultaneously is greatly simplified than it has been in traditional physical military warfare.

These examples are far from an exhaustive list of major trends that will reshape and reset the global economy over the next several decades. My intention isn't to articulate a definitive taxonomy of the wheels and gears turning underneath the hood of the world's economic machinery in the twenty-first century. Rather, I'm simply highlighting a few of the massive transitions that were already underway before the pandemic and that will continue to drive change long after the pandemic has receded out of the limelight.

Despite the challenges of the pandemic and these other trends changing the global economy, there's a growing awareness of both the importance and the realistic opportunity to rebuild the economy of India. But what exactly does it mean when we refer to the goal of "rebuilding India"? While some may frame this objective in terms of quantitative economic goals – e.g., driving X% of the global economy – our emphasis is on several more qualitative goals:

- Reestablishing India's prominence as a manufacturing hub for the world
- Playing a stronger role in driving innovation that transforms the global economy
- Ensuring that all the essential building blocks are in place to sustain this restored position in the global economy, including strong R&D capabilities in business and academia and forging government policies that are designed to support this long-term vision

When it comes to developing an action plan for rebuilding India, several themes have emerged as key areas that will determine whether the country succeeds in its ambitious goals, or if it will lag behind the aggressive gameplans exhibited by other countries. (And if we are to be honest with ourselves, there really is no such thing as "lagging behind" in today's competitive economy – those who "lag behind" for more than a cycle or two quickly become irrelevant.) The keys to successfully implementing growth markets in India are:

- Developing world class manufacturing capabilities built on a foundation of smart infrastructure
- Accelerating the development of 21st-century talent with digital platforms

- "Last-mile" connectivity that brings 1.4 billion people online to participate in global markets as merchants, consumers, employees, and entrepreneurs.

The critical nature of these keys to growth have been established as part of my previous research projects. These initiatives have included:

- The BIF, our ongoing series of gatherings of senior government and business leaders representing every facet of the Indian economic ecosystem
- Extensive research and field trials in the development of "smart villages" in India that create new economic opportunities both for residents of rural villages throughout the country as well as for global companies that invest in these opportunities
- The pioneering research in "open innovation," led by UC Berkeley's Henry Chesbrough, that I've been privileged to collaborate on from time to time. Open innovation is a highly effective process whereby organizations advance their own objectives by sharing research and development efforts that benefit all participants, a reflection of the maxim that "a rising tide lifts all boats."
- UC Berkeley's Rebuilding India Initiative, co-chaired by Dr. Rajiv Kumar, the co-chairman of NITI Aayog, a public policy think tank within the office of the Indian prime minister.
- Previous books that have helped to capture, consolidate, and catalyze these initiatives, including *The Road to Mori* (an overview of the smart village movement), *How to Create Smart Villages* (a workbook for participants in the smart village movement), *How to Think Like the CEO of the Planet* (a

guide for developing strategies for sustainability). A memoir – *The Untouchables* – offers some background on how my family's personal circumstances shaped my thinking on many of these topics.

In the chapters that comprise the bulk of this section, we'll provide a detailed action plan for members of each of the key groups of stakeholders – businesses, government officials, consumers, and academics – working to play a role in the process of rebuilding India. Their immediate objectives may be varied, but each group is likely working to achieve both personal success as well as success for the greater good of the country. As you'll see, these dual objectives are hardly in conflict with one another.

This edition has adopted a different approach to organizing these steps than its predecessor. That edition was organized to prompt dialogue across each of the four stakeholder groups on each of the five crucial ideas for building any economy in the 21st century. Our hope was to encourage conversations that, regardless of whatever conclusions they might reach (if any) would help to foster further trust among stakeholder groups, simply by virtue of promoting greater dialogue and surfacing concerns and ideas that might not be apparent to members of the other groups.

This edition assumes that stakeholders are well on their way toward strengthening relationships with other stakeholders and pursues the subsequent steps for taking concrete actions and achieving tangible outcomes. To that end, it is focused on three important steps on the path to rebuilding India:

- creating and leveraging smart infrastructure
- accelerating the development of 21st century talent
- providing last-mile connectivity to 1.4 billion people in India that will enable more robust participation in the new economy.

You may also notice that there are more contributions provided by business and government leaders (vs. representatives of academia and consumers), as there is greater diversity in the challenges and opportunities in those sectors to be explored.

Before diving into the step-by-step solutions offered for each of these objectives by each of the stakeholder groups, I'll provide a little background and context on each of these three challenges, outlining the nature of the challenge, why it's a critical sub-objective to support the overall objective of rebuilding India, what's been tried in the past, and some observations on what's worked – and what hasn't – in achieving these goals.

LAST-MILE CONNECTIVITY

The last-mile challenge refers to the intrinsic difficulty of distributing any kind of goods or services to individual end-users. A company may be able to successfully manufacture their product in a single location (or in a few locations) and deliver it to a distribution network of several (or several dozen, or even several hundred) local facilities. Once the item reaches a distribution hub, it may only be a very short distance from its ultimate destination, but completing that "last mile" of its journey from manufacture to customer can be exponentially more difficult than the previous 99.9% of its journey. (Our focus will be primarily on the last-mile challenges for Internet connectivity, but I'll use the example of last-mile distribution of physical goods to illustrate some of the general challenges of last-mile logistics.)

There are several reasons for this. First, it's a matter of simple mathematics. To borrow a metaphor from fractal mathematics, picture a fairly simple geometric structure – the blood vessels in a living animal, the roots of a plant, the coastline of a body of water, the petals on a flower. The closer you zoom in on your view of that structure, an increasingly complex level of detail is revealed. No matter how close you zoom in, the structure just keeps getting more and more complex.

A map of the journey of a product from creation to final delivery destination has a similar property; after traveling hundreds of miles to get within a mile of the end point, you might think the journey is basically done, only to discover it takes practically forever to travel that last mile. (If you've ever anxiously followed the progress of a UPS or FedEx delivery, you're probably familiar with this concept.)

Another reason why the last mile is the toughest is that there's often more variation among last miles than there is for the bulk of the journey. Manufacturing centers are often located at robust transportation hubs, so the first leg of the journey will take place using well-constructed and well-maintained shipping lanes, whether they're across land, water, or air. The next leg might find the item transferred to a regional transportation facility, which is still a well-designed and well-managed operation. But in reaching that last mile, all bets are off. Rather than a container ship, or a superhighway, the last mile might be an unpaved and unmarked dirt road. It may be indicated with a nonstandardized and unverified address. It may even fall outside the purview of Google Maps.

Finally, that final leg of the journey is often complicated by specific logistics considerations. Let's say the item being delivered requires refrigeration (like many foods, medicines, and other perishable items). That's generally not a problem for modern transportation facilities. But in the last mile, it can present untenable challenges.

Perhaps you've ordered ice cream to be delivered to your front door. The package is left at your gate, rather than your front door, where you don't notice it for several days. Or perhaps you've been out of town – only briefly, but too long for the dry ice packaging to keep your cookie dough ice cream intact. Maybe somebody steals the package for the brief window of time it's left unsecured. Perhaps there are ice cream-loving animals in your neighborhood.

These examples have referred to the last-mile challenges for delivery of physical goods. But today, last-mile connectivity of services – notably electricity and Internet access – have become at least as important as physical last-mile deliveries. The last-mile connectivity challenge shares many of the same obstacles as last-mile delivery of physical items:

- The magnitude of the number of final destinations is exponentially larger than the scale of the distribution network covers all but the last mile
- The external environment often introduces a host of complex one-off scenarios that must each be tackled
- Any special considerations that are relatively straightforward to address in the more manageable parts of a distribution network may be extremely hard to address in the last-mile. For example, just as refrigeration and other types of special handling may become impossible in the final mile, network security may be far more challenging in that last mile.

Why is last-mile connectivity essential?
The networking pioneer Bob Metcalfe made an observation that has come to be known as Metcalfe's Law. It states that each new addition to a network increases the value of that network by much more than a simple linear function. In other words, a network that

links 8 people is far more than twice as valuable as a network with 4 people. And a network with a billion people is far more than twice as valuable as a network with 500 million people.

It's pretty easy to intuitively see that this is the case. When one new person joins a network – whether it's a Slack group at work, or a Facebook sub-community, or someone getting an email address for the first time – they can now contribute in many ways that were previously impossible (or far more difficult). They can contribute ideas, provide feedback on other peoples' ideas, buy goods, sell services, or simply upload funny pictures of their pets. They accrue benefits themselves and they potentially provide benefits to every other member of that network. (One need only look at the market cap for Facebook itself to see how the marketplace has validated the idea behind Metcalfe's Law; Facebook may have its ups and downs, but it has created vast wealth for its investors.)

In the Indian economy, last-mile connectivity is a prerequisite for a long list of socially beneficial possibilities:

- Online education (from basic literacy to professional development)
- Buying and selling of goods, creating potential marketplaces beyond the local geography that many would otherwise be limited to
- Instant access to information that offers enormous benefits (such as weather data that farmers can use to improve crop yields)
- The ability to participate in political discourse and decisions more actively
- Access to healthcare services that might otherwise be unavailable

How has last-mile connectivity been approached in the past?

The advent of smartphones has provided a giant leap forward toward last-mile connectivity. Cellular networks can bypass many of the challenges of physical telephone cable networks. However, with the advent of 5G as the emerging new standard, the cell tower infrastructure may become a little more like older wired networks, in that the cell towers need to be spaced much closer to each other. (Fortunately, they are much smaller.)

The need for more – and more regularly spaced – towers may prove challenging. Connectivity also depends on reliable 24/7 sources of electricity, which can also be a tall order in many areas. Ultimately, citizens in villages and remote areas will often have limited Internet access. They may only be able to access the Internet at certain times of the day, or from a battery-powered phone (but not from a desktop computer). Those who take online access from a robust PC with multiple monitors for granted should understand that an online presence for a rural Indian may be something quite different.

DEVELOPING THE TALENT POOL FOR THE 21ST CENTURY

Last-mile connectivity has been a challenge for different industries for centuries (albeit with somewhat different challenges for things like shipping and transportation as opposed to Internet connectivity). In contrast, the next challenge – the current state of India's talent pool – presents a paradox that feels distinctly contemporary.

The country has a long track record of placing a premium on educating its people – and its workforce – with successful results. The country has had world class talent in many leading industries. The number of Nobel laureates born in India continues to be disproportionately high. In the digital era, the country has been a world leader in training and educating computer and data scientists. In the highly competitive realm of Silicon Valley, Indian-born entrepreneurs have an extremely strong presence, as executives, top technologists, and founders of many leading startups and global companies.

And yet, one of the most pressing issues for many innovative countries in India is the lack of suitable talent to fill the urgent need for countless open positions. Lack of appropriate knowledge, skills, and experience is cited as one of the main factors behind this shortfall. According to a 2018 report published by the Centre for Monitoring Indian Economy (CMIE), there were around 31 million unemployed Indians seeking jobs, the highest ever up until that point. And in 2020, unemployment levels were pegged at 7.11% in an analysis from the Centre for Economic Data and Analysis (https://www.moneycontrol.com/news/trends/indias-unemployment-rate-in-2020-highest-since-1991-report-6953491. html). This was up sharply from the rate for the previous year (5.27%). While the pandemic obviously accounted for some of this spike, the rate for India was significantly higher than the rates for neighboring countries.

A detailed quantitative assessment of the magnitude of the skills gap can be found in this analysis on ResearchGate: https://www.researchgate.net/publication/295598089_Estimating_India%27s_skill_gap_on_a_realistic_basis_for_2022. And while there may be some quibbling over the precise nature of the skills gap, there's near-unanimous agreement that it's a significant challenge for the Indian economy – and for individual workers. A recent survey (https://timesofindia.indiatimes.com/business/

india-business/92-of-employees-believe-india-suffers-from-skills-gap-study/articleshow/78293159.cms) of employees found that 92% believe the skills gap is a significant factor in holding back competitiveness, and expect their employers to support efforts to close the gap.

Others have examined the reasons for this gap in India's workforce. The key factors driving this gap appear to be that traditional training within traditional educational institutions hasn't evolved as quickly as the needs of the marketplace require (Unemployed workforce vs no skilled candidates – what challenges India the most? (yourstory.com)). Those interested in an overview of the Indian educational system (including vocational training) can find a comprehensive summary in this 2008 report from the Asian Development Bank (ADB): https://www.adb.org/sites/default/files/publication/159351/adbi-workforce-dev-india.pdf.

That same ADB report notes several other factors that have exacerbated the skills gap, including:

- A large disparity in the quality of education among different types of engineering institutions
- Insufficient links between academic institutions and the business world
- Even among graduates who are well trained in their engineering disciplines, there is often a lack of "soft skills" such as interpersonal communications and effective work habits
- A shortage of well-trained teachers
- Outdated curricula that fails to reflect the rapid pace of change in industrial technology
- A lack of monitoring, accountability, and equity in the institutions entrusted with training and education.

The ADB report also cites the dwindling level interest in pursuing advanced education and academic research programs, in favor of pursuing the job market: "Compared to 10,000 master's and 800 PhDs given out per year in computer science in the United States, only 300 master's in technology and 25 PhDs in computer science are produced per year in India. For the country to move up the value chain in the IT industry and become a power in knowledge-led business, it must give greater importance to postgraduate education and research."

Among the recommendations presented in the report, a key approach is the move toward so-called modular training: "The introduction of modular employable skills (MES) lies at the heart of the new skill development program. The concept of MES is based on the identification and development of a 'minimum skills set' which is sufficient to get employment in the labor market or to enable a person to earn a living through self-employment. The flexibility of such modular credit-based courses is likely to lead to better opportunities for skill upgrading, multiskilling, multi-point entry and exit, vertical mobility and recognition of prior learning through certification of skills acquired informally."

Sectors deploying modular training to date span a diverse range of industries including the production of khadi goods, agricultural machinery, electronics, and process engineering.

The 2009 National Policy on Skill Development was designed to improve the workforce's skills and knowledge, as well as internationally recognized qualifications, to boost employment levels and to improve global competitiveness. The goals of this policy are ambitious, and encompass a variety of tactics:

– Use of a demand-driven system to align development efforts with the needs of the labor market

- A variety of initiatives to expand outreach
- A National Vocational Qualifications Framework designed to enhance for ongoing general and technical education and certification of competencies regardless
- Greater inclusiveness within groups that have traditionally had less access to knowledge and training, including women, disabled people, and disadvantaged groups
- Targeting the needs of emerging occupations
- Creating greater opportunities for lifelong learning, including pre-employment training
- Updating approaches to training, including providing improved training for the trainers themselves

The policy applies to the full range of educational institutions, and also includes learning initiatives of different ministries and other government departments. It also encompasses formal and informal apprenticeships and other types of training programs managed by enterprises, as well as training for self-employment and entrepreneurial opportunities. The policy also applies to e-learning, web-based learning, and distance learning.

A more detailed overview of the policy can be found in the following report from the India Brand Equity Foundation: skilling-the-workforce.pdf (ibef.org). Additional details about workforce challenges in specific sectors and among specific labor demographics can be found here: (PDF) Estimating India's skill gap on a realistic basis for 2022 (researchgate.net).

Why the talent gap is a critical barrier to rebuilding India's economy
This gap is much more than a mere inconvenience, or a factor that increases costs for employers who find themselves paying a premium to attract scarce talent. Those are important factors, to be sure. But as this phenomenon persists, it also erodes India's

overall competitive potential on the global stage. A talent shortfall also translates into lagging behind when it comes to innovation in the development of new products and processes. It creates an environment in which companies are more likely to take a more conservative approach to manufacturing strategies, rather than risk pursuing new strategies that may flounder when they're unable to hire professionals with the skill sets needed to implement them.

When corporate talent lags, it also has a stifling effect on potential R&D initiatives within academia. Universities may have the right talent to pursue important innovations, but with no corporate counterparts to partner with, these possibilities may fizzle out before they can even get started. Similarly, this talent gap may lead government agencies to opt for less ambitious policies that aim to simply tread water rather than pursue new avenues.

What approaches have been pursued to close this gap?
As workers migrate from rural and predominantly agricultural sectors to other urban sectors, India has a pronounced need for a clear and well-executed strategy to provide a new set of skills through vocational training to effectively deploy this surge in the workforce and sustain economic growth. It is also necessary to also build a robust infrastructure of trainers and training programs to accomplish that goal.

Recognizing this need, the Indian government has pursued several initiatives such as:

- Setting up centers for vocational training for people in rural and urban areas
- The creation of a network for vocational training
- Launching various programs for the development of skills among workers, including a special Ministry of Skilling

focused on developing public policies and infrastructure related to skill development
- Identifying industries likely to experience growth in their workforce requirements

There have been different approaches pursued by the Indian government and other organizations. These have focused on the following areas:

- Gauging industry demand by assessing labor market signals to better balance skills with demand
- Expansion of outreach using both established and innovative approaches
- A National Vocational Qualifications Framework that will include opportunities for horizontal and vertical mobility between general and technical education, recognition and certification of competencies irrespective of mode of learning. In this framework, skills learned from small private skill providers that are not affiliated with any larger organization would be recognized alongside skills learned from educational institutions established by the government. (Most of the rural population participates in the former type of training program.)
- A system to deliver competencies in line with nationally and internationally recognized standards
- Pre-employment training and life-long learning for skills needed in emerging occupations, so that both individual workers and enterprises can thrive in a workplace experiencing an increasingly rapid pace of change by anticipating and building competencies for the future
- Adequate participation of women, disabled persons and disadvantaged groups in the workforce, including those in the Economically Weaker Section (EWS), a classification that

includes those with an annual family income of less than US$11,000. The goal is to enhance their access to training, thereby improving employability and increasing employment opportunities
- Greater emphasis on research, planning, and monitoring
- Encouraging involvement of social partners with responsibility for managing and financing of training centers among all stakeholders, creating a greater space for public-private partnerships (P-P-P)
- Promoting better use of more modern training technologies
- Improving skills of trainers, quality assurance, and improvement of economic status

These efforts will encompass a variety of learning modes and venues, including:

- Institution-based, including information and communications technology training facilities (known as ITCs), vocational schools, technical schools, polytechnics and professional colleges
- Learning initiatives of different ministries and departments
- Formal and informal apprenticeships and other types of training by businesses
- Training for self-employment or entrepreneurial development
- Adult learning and retraining of retired or retiring employees
- Informal training programmes, including those provided by civil society organizations
- E-learning, web-based learning and distance learning

The primary emphasis will be on:

- Sectors that will drive substantial employment, including textiles and garments, leather and footwear, gems

and jewelry, food processing industries, handlooms and handicrafts
- Sectors that will deepen technology capabilities in manufacturing, including machine tools, IT hardware, and electronics
- Sectors that will provide strategic security, such as telecommunications equipment, aerospace, shipping, and defense equipment
- Manufacturing technology sectors for energy security, including solar energy, clean coal technologies, and nuclear power generation
- Capital equipment for India's infrastructure growth, especially heavy electrical equipment, heavy transport, earth moving, and mining equipment
- Sectors in which India has a competitive advantage, including automotive sectors, pharmaceutical, and medical equipment
- Micro, small, and medium enterprises, which provide the base for the manufacturing sector by driving employment and enterprise generation

State governments and other stakeholders (such as industry associations, international organizations, and businesses) will also contribute by providing various types of financial aid and developing programs to assist in meeting these skill-development objectives.

WHAT'S WORKED AND WHAT HASN'T?

As we look to forge a path for rebuilding India, it's useful to examine what kinds of initiatives have been successful in the past, as well as what initiatives have stalled. These past experiences offer some valuable lessons that will be critical in planning a path forward for rebuilding India.

Building Smart Infrastructure
A new generation of smart infrastructure is an essential building block for a reinvigorated future for India as a manufacturing hub for the world.

What makes infrastructure smart? Smart infrastructure delivers value in several possible ways:

- It can provide greater value than previous generations of infrastructure by delivering additional features and benefits
- It can require less maintenance and oversight by monitoring itself and proactively providing alerts (and possibly even fixes) when it detects out-of-line conditions
- It can accommodate future innovation without requiring extensive retooling, relying more on software updates rather than hardware replacement
- It can deliver these enhancements at a lower cost, with a longer lifespan, and with greater reliability

A variety of technologies can help provide the intelligence that makes infrastructure smarter. For example:
- Systems that leverage artificial intelligence and machine learning can anticipate costly breakdowns before they happen, recommending maintenance actions that can be taken to prevent problems that would otherwise be likely to occur
- By leveraging the fast-growing "Internet of Things" (networked devices in manufacturing and other industrial environments), complex and geographically distributed facilities can more easily be managed from a central control hub
- "Big data" systems that consolidate massive amounts of information from a broad array of sources can be leveraged to identify patterns, trends, and analytics that drive greater efficiencies

In many regards, this goal overlaps with and supports the other two goals of closing the talent gap and providing last-mile connectivity. Last-mile connectivity can, in a sense, be thought of as one pillar of the smart infrastructure needed to rebuild India. And smart infrastructure also provides a mechanism for at least partially compensating for occasional gaps in the talent pool by relying on infrastructure that can guide workers to the right outcomes.

Why smart infrastructure matters

Some of the benefits of smart infrastructure should be self-evident. Although deploying smarter infrastructure may require an upfront investment, that capital investment will quickly be paid back in the form of reduced operating expenses that continue to generate benefits far into the future.

But there are also some less obvious benefits that make smart infrastructure an important priority. A company that is always focused on dealing with a never-ending series of infrastructure failures will have a hard time devoting much attention to the important business of innovation. This is especially critical in the wake of crises such as a global pandemic, economic turmoil, and supply chain disruptions, where innovation isn't merely a nice-to-have goal, but has become an essential part of the day-to-day fabric when companies are forced to reinvent themselves – their products, their customers, their logistics, their supply chain, their markets – on a frequent basis. Smarter infrastructure provides a foundation for businesses to operate with far greater resiliency in the face of an increasingly uncertain set of standard operating procedures.

There is no longer such a thing as "business as usual," and smart infrastructure allows companies to work within this new reality.

What smart infrastructure initiatives have been attempted to date?

A country rises or falls on its infrastructure. The Indian government recognizes this and has a number of ongoing projects to enhance India's infrastructure. The National Infrastructure Pipeline (NIP) for FY 2019-2025 is a first-of-its-kind, whole-of-government exercise to provide world-class infrastructure designed to boost the economy, attract investment in infrastructure, and improve overall quality of life. To draw up the NIP, a High-Level Task Force was constituted as a program within the Ministry of Finance. The NIP was created on a best-efforts basis by aggregating information from various stakeholders including line ministries, departments, state governments, and private sector stakeholders across infrastructure sub-sectors.

Allocating over 103 lakh crores for infrastructure projects including roads, highways, railways, airports, and ports, the government has identified over 6,500 projects under the NIP with the goal of building a $5 trillion economy by 2025.

While many of these announcements came before the COVID-19 crisis hit India, they are even more relevant – and have assumed a higher priority – in a crisis with a deepening financial crunch and staggering economies. Government infrastructure spending could create jobs, increase purchasing power, and generate consumer demand to revive the economy. Infrastructure spending directly drives related sectors such as cement, steel, and diesel, accelerating the overall pace of the economy.

Here are a few government infrastructure development initiatives and avenues for financing construction projects:

Roads and Highways: In 2017, the Indian government, approved a total investment of around $US 95 billion for the construction of over 83,677 km of roads in the following five years. The FY2021 budget also provided for capital for accelerated development of roads and highways.

The Investment Information and Credit Rating Agency of India (ICRA) expects roughly 9,000 km of road projects to be executed over 2019-2025, initially at a pace 10% lower than in previous years as a result of COVID-19. However, by July, 2020, there were early signs of recovery. For example, toll collections across national highways had risen to 87% of pre-COVID levels. Enhanced spending on construction of roads and highways increases the demand for construction and mining equipment, laborers, and more, which helps put cash directly in citizens' hands.

Foreign Direct Investment (FDI): In a move to attract more foreign investments in the infrastructure sector, the government has relaxed several FDI regulations to allow 100% FDI investment in select construction development projects. Moreover, these new provisions have also eliminated the lock-in period of three years (during which funds could not be taken back) in specific real estate development projects such as hotels and tourist resorts and hospitals, a move intended to make such projects more attractive to high net-worth individuals.

Lack of international financing has been a significant limiting factor in improving infrastructure in India (and many other developing countries). While relaxing these restrictions will undoubtedly attract more foreign investment, construction financing also offers businesses another viable financing option, rather than waiting to accumulate the necessary capital ahead of time. Increasing construction finance loans could speed up infrastructure development plans without burdening cashflow for those driving the projects.

Smart Cities: To accelerate urban infrastructure, the Indian government has articulated a vision of developing 100 smart cities starting in 2015. The Government allocated INR 6,450 crore in its 2020 budget to develop five such smart cities in the fiscal year FY2021. While COVID-19 might have delayed this initiative's progress, the urbanization endeavor would create jobs and boost economic growth across identified states.

These projects require huge upfront investment that could be accommodated by accessing builder finance. For example, Tata Capital allows for flexibility in such loans that can be tailored to match the government's milestone payouts to ensure loan repayments align with income, an approach that would facilitate many projects that remain in limbo while the developers seek the necessary upfront capital.

Transport: In the Union Budget 2020-21, the government has given a massive push by allocating INR 1.70 trillion for transport infrastructure. Of the 103 lakh crore invested in NIP projects, over 37 lakh crore is estimated to upgrade transportation, including metro, rails, airports, and ports. The government also plans to build 100 airports by 2024 and launch more Tejas trains to promote tourism and domestic travel. (The Tejas Express is a semi-high-speed fully air-conditioned train Introduced by Indian Railways. It features modern onboard facilities such as doors that operate automatically. Tejas is an Indian word that can mean "sharp", "luster," and "brilliance," adjectives that these trains aim to embody.)

Power: The power sector is one of the keys to propel economic growth in the country, and the Union Budget 2020-21 allocated Rs 22000 crores for discom reforms, power, and renewable energy sector. To further push India's renewable energy capacity, the government also plans to establish a renewable energy capacity of

500 GW by 2030, including large solar power plants along railway tracks.

Oil & Gas: Under the Open Acreage Licensing Policy (OALP), 1.37 lakh sq km have been allocated to the private sector and central public sector enterprises for exploration. There is also a plan for a 51% expansion of the national gas distribution grid to 2,7000 km.

In light of the pandemic, a few other measures taken by the government to continue its momentum in infrastructure development are:

– The National Highway Authority of India is able to accelerate payments for projects as a result of a loosening of the required milestones before payouts can be made
– Compensation for loss of toll collection by increasing the concession periods (a grace period offered to contractors if they don't finish work as originally scheduled)
– All registered real estate projects and central departments – including railways, public works department, ministry of road, transport, and highways – have offered an extension of time of at least 90 days and up to 180 days to all undergoing projects without any penalty
– Government agencies to release retention of payments proportionately to the extent contracts are completed to provide greater working capital for road contractors
– Speedy settlement of arbitration of disputes between government and contractors

What's worked and what hasn't?
India's Smart Cities Mission (SCM) identified 100 cities, covering 21% of India's urban population, for a makeover in four rounds

starting January 2016 (see the following table). Each smart city is expected to complete its projects within five years from the date of selection. These projects are meant to improve core infrastructure and services to make cities more liveable, economically vibrant and environmentally sustainable.

However, 49% of 5,196 projects for which work orders were issued across 100 smart cities in India remain unfinished, as per government data. Among 33 cities which completed their five-year duration this year, 42% projects are incomplete.

Progress Of Projects Under Smart Cities Mission

Round	Commencement date	Number of cities	Projects Completed
One	January 2016	20	65%
Fast Track	May 2016	13	40%
Two	September 2016	27	54%
Three	June 2017	30	33%
Four	January 2018	10	35%

Note: Data as of 10 a.m. on June 23. Data for New Delhi, Naya Raipur, Bhubaneswar and Salem are as of January 2021, as submitted to the Rajya Sabha. Source: Smart Cities dashboard, Ministry of Housing & Urban Affairs

Institutional and structural issues with the special purpose vehicles (SPVs) – public-private partnerships tasked with implementing the mission – include funding roadblocks, understaffed and unskilled manpower, and the lack of citizen participation, according to urban planners and analysts sharing their view with IndiaSpend (the "agency of record" for data about the Indian social and political economy, particularly in areas such as education and healthcare). They also criticized the mission for not incorporating "sustainable" and "inclusive" factors into its development plans, as we address later.

In 2019, around 470 million people lived in Indian cities, about a third of the country's total population. India's urban population is expected to rise to 38.6% by 2026. Rapid urbanization will then pose even bigger challenges related to waste management, air pollution, traffic congestion, scarce resources and more. Smart cities were envisioned to be a solution to these concerns.

Overambitious plans
The mission has often been criticized for being too ambitious. For example,

- Many cities have proposed projects that exceed their capacity in terms of both financial and human resources.
- Seed funding from the government offers a starting point, but it still needs to be enhanced by funding from other sources (such as taxes on entertainment and sanitation services, parking fees, or loans from banks and international institutions such as the World Bank).
- Bureaucratic complexity and resistance among stakeholders can create unexpected delays and bottlenecks. And the lack of simultaneous commitment from stakeholders often prevents individual stakeholders from moving forward. As different groups of stakeholders operate in different timeframes and on different schedules, it can become impossible to coordinate activities that need to take place simultaneously for a successful implementation.

Budget Constraints
A 2018 study by the Centre for Policy Research (CPR), a Delhi-based think-tank, across 99 smart cities showed that about 70% of

funds were sourced from public sources, some 25% from PPP initiatives and corporate social responsibility (CSR) funds, 5% from
loans and 1% from user charges.

Apart from the current global economic downturn, certain flaws
in the mission's model have made it difficult for the municipal
corporation to raise and utilize funds. Some charged that public
assets owned by the municipal corporations were transferred to
the SPVs and the SPVs sold these properties at market rates. The
resulting profits may have created distortions in the market.

In interviews with 13 government officers and seven industrial pro-
fessionals/consultants for a 2019 case study conducted by Virginia
Polytechnic Institute and State University on two smart cities,
Kakinada in Andhra Pradesh and Kanpur in Uttar Pradesh, "budget constraints" and "designing financially infeasible projects"
were the most frequent complaints.

The interviewees also highlighted "delay in payments" to contractors and "distrust among private players towards city agencies" in
explaining why the SCM falls short of the expectations for private
investments.

Similarly, smart city Indore faced a scarcity of funds as private companies refrained from investing in projects whose high revenue
demands (recovery costs) were to be met by user charges – citizens
had to pay for the high maintenance and operation costs but were
unable to do so. Chennai and Ludhiana also faced issues of limited
funding that hindered their progress, as per a 2018 report by Housing
and Land Rights Network (HLRN) India, a charitable trust.

In other words, a common pattern often emerges: Money is bud-
geted, a process for distributing it is developed, but administrative

clutter results in the program's stagnation. Some cities received no funding, others found their funding delayed. Furthermore, as various government officials change roles, there is a lack of continuity for these projects that often require long-term oversight.

This structure has also led to delays in project implementation through the private sector with projects getting stuck in the tendering stage where a project analysis has to be jointly done by the SPV, the State Planning Board, and the state government, as per the Indore case study.

Furthermore, employees of the SPVs also work for the municipality and this creates friction between the private partners and government officials, said an industry professional interviewed for the Kakinada and Kanpur case study. For instance, Chennai SPV includes 11 officials from the Tamil Nadu government as board of directors, and of the five non-official members (including the CEO) only two are independent directors, per the HLRN report.

Lack of Urban Planners

India is expected to fall short of 1.1 million urban planners by 2020, IndiaSpend reported in April 2018. "On the issue of shortage of town planners, the Committee feel that the 5,500, town planners who are working under the Mission with ULBs is too less," according to a March, 2018, Parliamentary Standing Committee report.

Increasing Disparities

Other flaws in the program have also surfaced. In many cases, only a small percentage of a city's population will benefit from the mission. Among area-based urban development projects, only 0.8% of Pune's population will benefit, with similarly low numbers for Ahmedabad (1.5%), Bhopal (1.7%), Ludhiana (2.2%), Patna (2.3%), Aurangabad (2.4%), and Lucknow (2.5%), the

Ministry of Housing and Urban Affairs told Rajya Sabha in July, 2017. Cities where a high percentage of the population benefits include Port Blair (77%), Namchi (74%), Vellore and Pasighat (63%), Thane (57%), and Dharamshala (51%). In addition, 28 of 99 smart cities do not mention any steps towards the marginalized and low-income groups in their proposals, per the HLRN 2018 report.

Lack of "Smart Citizens" and Sustainability not a Priority
Smart city proposals lay emphasis on digital outreach and feedback through MyGov websites, Facebook, Twitter, and other channels. But India's digital divide could further exclude the marginalized from the process. Only 40 of the top 60 cities had provided information on the exact number of people consulted through a non-digital medium, and only 24 mentioned inputs received – but mostly from limited public consultations – according to the CPR analysis. The absence of a "smart citizen" – someone who embraces the ideas expressed in the quadruple helix model and who has a substantial level of trust in the other stakeholder groups – in the equation further stifles the mission's progress. For example, in waste management, along with using smart technologies such as GPS tracking devices for city sweepers, the relationship between the waste collector and waste generator is fundamental. Smart cities are focused more on creating accomplished infrastructure such as large-scale plants but not on the relationship between the waste collector and generator. This relationship needs to be mended to validate the costly infrastructure and improve sustainability.

No city has prioritized smart environments over other dimensions, according to a policy analysis by Telematics and Informatics, an interdisciplinary journal. A break-down of the smart environment dimension showed that 17 smart cities have strategized to focus on cleanliness and clean energy. The second-most prioritized sub-dimensions in 16 cities are improvement in air quality and establishing sustainable infrastructure that includes solid-waste treatment, renewable sources of energy, public toilets, and green cover.

What Else Is on the Critical Path for Rebuilding India?

These key issues – closing the talent gap, establishing widespread last-mile connectivity, and creating a new generation of smart infrastructure – are important building blocks for rebuilding India. Are they the only critical steps to reach this objective? Probably not. Is it possible that the goals of rebuilding India, such as reestablishing the country as the manufacturing hub for the global economy, can be achieved without first accomplishing these foundational preliminary goals? Perhaps.

Over the course of the research and dialogues that informed this book, other goals and tactics surfaced, and these are discussed in the chapters that follow. And perhaps there are other tactics that you feel are essential steps for India's revitalization.

But while other tactics could emerge that have a higher priority than these three, there's also a slightly hidden agenda behind these three: Each of them requires a vigorous level of dialogue across the four stakeholder groups discussed earlier. That dialogue will play a major role in increasing the level of trust among and across the stakeholder groups. And fostering that trust – as discussed in detail in *Resetting the Jewel in the Crown* – may well be an even more valuable outcome than any of these three goals.

Without a more robust degree of trust, none of the goals can be successfully implemented. And with an elevated level of trust, any additional goals that might be surfaced can be tackled far more easily.

We asked our guests at the BIF several key questions to help us understand their perspectives:

1. Our book offers a plan of action for rebuilding India, particularly in light of the COVID-19 pandemic, embracing three main tactics: providing universal last-mile connectivity, closing the talent gap, and developing smart infrastructure. Can you provide an example of an approach to achieve one of these goals that you think has worked well?
2. Can you provide an example of an approach to one of these goals that you think has stumbled?
3. What activities are you currently involved in that support these three tactics (or the broader goal of rebuilding India)?
4. Building greater trust across different groups of people is an essential first-step for achieving any of these goals. Do you have an example of something you or your organization has done that has successfully built a stronger degree of trust with other stakeholder groups?
5. How likely (as a percentage) do you think it is that India can reestablish itself as the manufacturing hub for the rest of the world by 2030?
6. Same question, but by 2050?
7. By what year do you feel confident that there's a 75% chance that India will have regained its prominence as a manufacturing hub to the world?

INSIGHTS FROM THE BERKELEY INNOVATION FORUM INDIA

IN MARCH OF 2022, leaders from global corporations, government agencies, academic researchers, and others gathered at the Center for Growth Markets at UC Berkeley for an event hosted by the Berkeley Innovation Forum and the NITI Aayog.

The forum included presentations of strategies and action plans to advance the initiatives associated with reinvigorating India's role as a global manufacturing hub along with vigorous discussions among the attendees. The remarks from this forum are shared as a snapshot from that particular time, as verbatim remarks that offer anecdotal insights and a variety of perspectives. The forum was conducted under Chatham House Rules, a common practice for this type of forum whereby the ideas expressed are intended to be freely shared, although the identities of the speakers (aside from the forum organizers) are shielded in any public discussion of the dialogue, such as this book. This is intended to instill a degree of confidentiality that is conducive to open and frank discussion.

In addition to the formal agenda, several attendees also took part in follow-up sessions during which they weighed in with their responses to a wide range of polling questions. The goal was to identify topics for which there was a substantial consensus vs. topics for which there was not a sense of conventional wisdom or for which appropriate solutions may not yet have been formulated. An analysis of those conclusions appears after a summary of the presentations and discussions at the forum.

One of the prevailing conclusions that emerged from the forum was the broad support for the goal for India to reclaim its status as a leader in global manufacturing. The commitment to that goal was expressed in different ways, but there was a common thread of enthusiasm underlying the presentations and discussions.

In his opening remarks at the forum, Professor Darwin made the following observation:

> It is pathetic that we run Silicon Valley where its value creation reaches the distant extremities of the world, but we are unable to run India. We have the vision, the passion, the knowledge, and the aspirational youth to drive our country forward but we are lacking alignment and collaborative approaches within our own ecosystem to lead the world. We were once the jewel that drew nations that created value for themselves; this time we will also create the value for the world but capture some of it for ourselves to sustain India and bless the world.

He subsequently provided an overview of the findings to date for the Rebuilding India Initiative, along with some goals for and outcomes from the forum:

> The Rebuilding India Initiative is about building an ecosystem based on trust to enable a scalable and sustainable business expansion for the Indian economy. We at Berkeley are taking the well-researched and validated approach to taking India forward. We plan to utilize the Triple-Helix and Open Innovation approaches that are responsible for the creation of the Silicon Valley ecosystem and allow it to thrive by creating value through technological interventions and job creation around the world.

The Triple-Helix approach incorporates three entities working together: 1) government, 2) universities, and 3) businesses. The U.S. government over the years has been the first mover and stakeholder by funding knowledge creation through universities and research institutions. That knowledge is consumed by businesses to create products and services to expand markets. The government has been paid back handsomely in return through job creation by taxpayers. This model worked well to prime the growth of the U.S. economy by attracting the brightest minds around the world to create value.

The United States established an environment of trust, equity, and merit (clearly articulated in its mission statement) and was largely responsible for the ensuing prosperity. The government has the capacity to understand the incentives, interests, and concerns of different stakeholders within the ecosystem to create win-win value propositions for rebuilding India. These value propositions, from the policy standpoint, need to be flexible to address the unique needs of various industries, individual firms, and geographic locations. Only the government can create a level playing field where everyone can prosper and thrive.

The second and parallel approach we intend to utilize is Open Innovation as the driver of knowledge distribution across the ecosystem to fuel growth. We plan to do this through the Berkeley Innovation Forum in India. This is where key CEOs, policymakers, and academics (researchers and creators of knowledge solutions) meet to dialogue on a regular basis to create value for all stakeholders in real time to accelerate solutions where needed. Knowledge is useless unless it flows.

Forums led by an agnostic orchestrator, like UC Berkeley, are essential to accelerate the process. Entities, by nature, like to hang on to their knowledge, not realizing that today's knowledge is useless tomorrow. The value of knowledge assets evaporates rapidly, unlike physical assets, as new knowledge is being created 24/7 around the world. For this reason, collaboration and exchange of knowledge and know-how are essential for growth.

Today, 90% of our balance sheets are composed of knowledge assets as opposed to when I was in college, when 90% of the assets were physical assets, like land, buildings, and equipment whose value created sustainable growth. Thus, our business models need to be built on knowledge rivers and not on knowledge lakes. This requires new methods to both scale and sustain our businesses.

Creating alignment between the government, universities, and businesses requires dynamic leadership capabilities. Leaders with dynamic capabilities need to orchestrate the symphony of diverse stakeholders within the business ecosystems.

Dynamic leaders bring people together to pull in the same direction; such leaders need to be identified and placed in key roles to shepherd the process. Alignment across industries eliminates costs from business ecosystems, saves time, and accelerates solutions where needed by rapid deployment.

The two approaches introduced earlier are what we plan to implement through the Berkeley Innovation Forum in India by bringing all three stakeholders (government, academics, and businesses) together to take India forward.

Next Steps: Over the past two years we have demonstrated that there is an appetite among the corporate sector to meet under one roof with government officials to discuss pain points across industries. Our first meeting in 2020 chaired by the NITI Aayog was attended by more than 40 firms that demonstrated an interest to work together on the Rebuilding India Initiative. In the interim, COVID has delayed our meetings.

However, our first-ever India in-person meeting on March 25-26, 2022, was attended by 30 firms. More than 18 firms attended the follow-up meeting with Dr. Rajiv Kumar to finish the discussions that you started at the earlier meetings. This demonstrates that you all value this forum and indicated so unanimously on the survey taken at the end of our meeting on March 26.

The 2022 forum began with a keynote speech from NITI Aayog vice chairman Dr. Rajiv Kumar. Next came a series of table discussions on three major initiatives: making India a global manufacturing hub, improving the country's digital education programs, and bringing internet connectivity to all parts of the nation. After Professor Darwin presented the results of a survey on the attendees' business priorities, the participants crafted action plans for each of the three objectives and presented them to Dr. Kumar, who responded with follow-up questions to be further discussed as next steps.

The event closed with speeches by Dr. Kumar and UC Berkeley representatives Werner Fischer and Yashraj Bhardwaj. What follows includes summaries of the key takeaways derived from the discussions, dialogue, and surveys at the forum, followed by a more detailed description of each portion of the event as well as the individual submissions that were used to generate the overall action plans for the three initiatives.

Major Barriers to Growth as expressed by the Participating Firms (based on the survey taken during the forum):

- Talent acquisition is the biggest bottleneck for business growth.
- Last-mile connectivity is a major challenge to expand markets.
- Collaborations through Open Innovation are needed for impact on business success.

- Alignment through ecosystem formation is of the highest priority for scalability and sustainability of business.
- Leadership capabilities are needed to orchestrate and navigate the necessary skills going forward.
- Consistency in policies is critical for the Triple-Helix approach to work.

INITIATIVE 1: MAKE INDIA A GLOBAL MANUFACTURING HUB ON PAR WITH CHINA

- **Unlock Sustainability as a Growth Driver.** India needs to invest in forthcoming technology that can turn the country into the hydrogen hub of the world. India can power growth through renewable energy while exporting its technology, rather than importing technology alongside energy.
- **Improve Cost Competitiveness through Academia/ Industry Collaborations.** Creating win-win academia-industry collaboration can accelerate research on cost-competitive solutions for sectors such as renewable energy, supply chain logistics, and policymaking:
  o Accelerating renewable energy growth lets the industry benefit from low-cost energy production.
  o Scaling of multimodal movement of goods through rail and coastal shipping reduces supply chain costs as compared to the road.
  o Reducing regulations minimizes affiliated regulatory costs for the industry
- **Intensify R&D to Grow OEMs.** Leaders in industry, academia, and the government need to facilitate increased innovation activities to launch best-in-class products. Investment in original design and R&D needs to be

increased to shift Indian manufacturing from assembly of foreign components to original equipment and component manufacturing.

- **Simplify Governance and Improve Ease of Doing Business.** Have a single-window clearance system for approvals in place. All the requirements should be made transparent and available to apply and comply to improve the ease of doing business. State-specific operationalization might be required as PAN India standardization has limitations.
- **Nurture Alignment & Trust.** Transforming ambitions into successful outcomes can only happen if trust between the government and the corporate sector is created as a foundation for innovation. Alignment should come from a mission mode.
- **Develop Industry Clusters.** Designing an ecosystem cluster approach for different industries where many smaller players can co-exist helps with just-in-time approaches, reduced supply chain cost, better efficiency, and synergy effects to push manufacturing growth. Ensure that components (e.g., chips) are manufactured in India, allowing bigger players to come there.

INITIATIVE 2: EMPOWER 600 MILLION ASPIRATIONAL YOUTH VIA DIGITAL PLATFORMS THROUGH ACCELERATED TALENT AND SKILL DEVELOPMENT

- **Facilitate Industry Engagement.** Engagement with industry is essential for academic curricula development, training of faculty, and providing students exposure to real-life knowledge application. This is to ensure well-trained students can be hired without further training.

- **Ensure Scalability of Digital Education.** There are many pilots in the educational field that can lead to tremendous impact and benefit, but somehow industry is not able to move beyond a handful of universities and a few thousand students. There is so much demand for further, speedy scaling, and the government is needed to facilitate scale because the educational system is complex, scattered, and highly regulated.
- **Move Toward Education 2.0.** India is ready for a new digital revolution (such as the much-trumpeted metaverse) that has the potential to create 10 times more value compared to today. That, however, requires more interdisciplinary, dynamic education to unlock new thinking:
  o Change the student testing paradigm. Education should be for skills, not for a degree.
  o Encourage students to question the status quo.
  o Push sustainability of education. The central government should provide the basic architecture while industry, academia, and government bodies test and launch innovative educational programs.
  o Ease of doing business needs to be applied to education to minimize the complexity of regulations while ensuring trust through robust systems.
- **Establish a Digital Hub Structure.** Digital platforms need to become more comprehensive and scalable. Open Innovation can make this happen to create a GitHub for education that allows flexible up- and reskilling, providing equal opportunities and democratizing education.
- **Ease Credit Accreditation.** Enable universal recognized micro-credentialing coming directly from commercial needs for skills that are quickly evolving. Learners' mobility should be appreciated through a multidisciplinary and dynamic credit system to let learners be more flexible.

- **Establish Benchmarking for Success.** Benchmarking success will help to identify successful programs that can be supported for scaling with state and local governments. The NITI Aayog is very open to designing those required metrics together with the industry.

INITIATIVE 3: BRING RURAL PEOPLE ONLINE VIA DIGITAL PLATFORMS TO SPEED UP TRADE, SAVE TIME, AND ELIMINATE MIDDLEMEN AND COST REDUNDANCIES

- **Understand Digital Connectivity as the Driver for Inclusive Growth.** Digital connectivity can allow us to tap into a $3 trillion opportunity when logistics and market linkages can create new value. New human benefits arise when mobilizing people and forming communities through connectivity. Success factors are:
  o Affordability
  o Gender equality and empowerment of women
  o Rural entrepreneurship
  o Faster rollout of wireless networks, leading to quicker benefits
  o Sufficient spectrum to create a quality network and sufficient capacity to support all use cases
- **Ensure Goal Alignment and Mission Mode.** Local communities, companies, and local, state and central bodies might have different goals and need to be aligned. Once all of them are part of one mission, digital connectivity to all households can be achieved within the next 3-5 years.
- **Tear Down Barriers.** To accelerate traction and consumer adoption:

o Access could be granted as a fundamental right (for free) while consumption charges could pay back investment later.

o Spectrum flexibility to increase bandwidth and quality for ensuring inclusiveness and growth. Severe language barriers and digital literacy issues can be eradicated through AI requiring high bandwidth.

o Smartphone penetration needs to further grow through affordable devices.

o The cost of laying fiber needs to be brought down through innovation.

• **Ensure Utilization and Commercial Value.** Use cases need to be applicable and create value for the individual and society to ensure that utilization of fiber unlocks commercial growth. Therefore, all efforts and initiatives need to be defined with specific metrics to ensure impact.

• **Deploy Effective Policies and Government Support.** Create reformative systems for policies and government support:

o Policies to allow easy investment in stakeholders to keep digital connections alive (e.g., health insurance in remote areas backed by digital solutions).

o Creating an infrastructure map and making this map available to private and public sectors to find and link communities, industries, and governments to help form policies, create alignment, and unlock new innovations that are scalable.

o Government to enable the creation of infrastructure through various partners rather than building it themselves; align goals and facilitate infrastructure building through the private sector.

o Provide viability gap funding in the initial stage before use cases become commercially viable.

A BRIEF HISTORY OF THE REBUILDING INDIA INITIATIVE

The Center for Growth Markets, UC Berkeley, under the leadership of its faculty director, Ganesh Iyer, and its executive director, Solomon Darwin, established the Rebuilding India Initiative in 2020 as a response to the raging COVID-19 pandemic. More than 40 leaders from industry, academia, and the government met for two days online to discuss ideas for establishing India as a global manufacturing hub, accelerating skill development, and building ecosystems to mitigate pandemic risks. As a response to the success of that initial meeting, UC Berkeley and the NITI Aayog joined forces for the Rebuilding India Initiative in early 2021 by signing a five-year MoU. The honorable Dr. Rajiv Kumar, Vice-Chair of the NITI Aayog, took the Chair for the Berkeley Innovation Forum India that serves as the platform for the Rebuilding India Initiative. In 2022, the prestigious group met for the first time physically in New Delhi at the Berkeley Innovation Forum India to build upon previous discussions (see Key Takeaways from 2020 section) and develop action plans for further implementation, as discussed in the remainder of this chapter.

Key Takeaways from 2020

Initiative 1: Establish India as the Second Manufacturing Hub for Diversified Global Supply Chains

- **Benefiting from the application of technology:** Participants extensively discussed the positive impacts of the application of technology within the manufacturing sector. The benefits of using technology in smart manufacturing can impact the remaining takeaways, including the importance of sustainability, the role of trust, engagement with academic institutions, and facilitating legislation, as stated below.

- **Importance of sustainability:** All companies highlighted the vital importance of sustainability, particularly within the manufacturing and energy sectors. In line with the government initiatives, major players within the Indian economy expressed their desire to engage in different activities of the sustainable value chain.

- **Role of trust within the global ecosystem:** Considering the global concerns and opportunities, including the impact of COVID-19 on corporates and SMEs across different sectors, the growing presence of China, and the close relationship between India and leading economies, including the U.S., all participants highlighted the opportunity for India to achieve a higher share of the global market as a leading manufacturer and reliable supplier.

- **Engagement and partnership with leading academic institutions** is necessary to accelerate solutions and knowledge creation through evidenced-based and implementable use cases.

- **Facilitating the legislative process:** India has long been an interesting market for corporate firms, as well as SMEs, looking to improve their market position. To improve India's position in the global value chain and facilitate the entrance of multiple firms into different sectors, a re-evaluation of the legislative process, particularly for new firms aiming to expand into the Indian market, remains of high importance.

Initiative 2: Develop Digital Infrastructure for Early Education and Skill Development for Job Creation

- **Government support for utilizing early education:** Includes a clear plan for infrastructure development, particularly in rural areas. To that aim, providing electricity, ease of access to the Internet at a low cost, and cellular support such as 3G and 4G remains necessary. Doing so will enable early educators to have access to high-quality materials.

- **Government support for utilizing higher education:** Calls for a clear strategic plan to partner with leading technology firms, including IBM, Microsoft, Adobe, Salesforce, SAP, and others, to provide IT training for higher education as well as recent graduates looking for recruitment. Doing so will enable future talent to develop their skills in cutting-edge technologies, including AI, machine learning, blockchain, cloud computing, and application programming.
- **Government support for NGOs:** Calls for a clear strategic plan that enables NGOs, charitable institutes, and non-profit funding bodies to have access to technological platforms that facilitate support for early and higher education.
- **Partnership with research entities:** Includes collaboration with leading institutions to conduct high-quality research that offers managerial and academic impact.

Initiative 3: Build Ecosystems in Key Sectors to Mitigate Pandemic Risk

- **Solutions must be future proof in terms of health, economy, and society:** Pandemics such as COVID-19 both affect people's health and result in social and economic problems. Solutions should be prepared for these situations and should contribute to social and economic welfare.
- **The power of accessibility, affordability, and scale:** To bridge the gap between rural and urban areas, healthcare, food, and financial systems need to be accessible, affordable, and scalable. These three aspects are related and should be considered together when developing innovations for rural

Indian citizens. Many examples can be found that demonstrate it is possible to combine the three elements, but collaboration is key. Public-private partnerships are critical for these elements because it is impossible to realize the complex requirements for innovation in rural areas through only one company.

- **Education is important at individual, organization, and ecosystem levels:** Education needs to take place at different levels to enable the realization of value co-creation. Individual members need the required (vocational) training to be able to do their jobs, but organizations also need to learn. Within organizations, the required knowledge of structures and processes must be in place to enable efficient learning processes and capture value. Education is also important to creating awareness in rural areas of the opportunities that being connected can offer in terms of quality of life.

- **Digitalization can create a quality of life for people in rural areas:** Digital technologies can improve the lives of many people living in rural areas because they can reduce costs and enhance scale. Farmers need to be connected to the market to get good prices. Rural citizens need to be connected to access affordable healthcare and to be financially included. The microlevel has to integrate technology to improve the quality of life for rural people and to bridge the gap between the urban and rural areas.

THE FORUM BEGINS

THE INVITED CEOS, government officers and heads of elite global firms were asked to form more efficient partnerships and ecosystems to take the Rebuilding India Initiative forward. Their mission was to begin building a collaborative action plan for each of the three initiatives involving all key stakeholders:

1. Make India a global manufacturing hub on par with China.
2. Empower 600 million aspirational youth via digital platforms to accelerate talent and skill development.
3. Bring rural people online via digital platforms to speedup trade, save time, and eliminate middlemen and cost redundancies.

The participants in each of the three initiatives were to identify and address the bottlenecks and the weakest links in the system to formulate solutions through collaborative engagement. They needed to develop win-win strategies to benefit all stakeholders within the ecosystems where needed. The role of each chair was to engage with their group in "matchmaking" among ecosystem players to develop a rough action plan for their initiatives.

Award Ceremony for Dr. Rajiv Kumar
After a team of senior Berkeley representatives, including Richard Lyons (Chief Innovation and Entrepreneurship Officer for the university) and Chris Bush (Executive Director of the Institute for Business Innovation at the Haas School of Business), welcomed the attendees, the conference dialogues and discussions began. On behalf of the Haas School of Business, UC Berkeley, and the Center for Growth Markets, Dr. Ganesh Iyer presented an award for distinguished contribution to leadership in innovation to Dr. Rajiv Kumar, Vice Chair of the NITI Aayog. Serving the largest democracy in the world, Dr. Kumar is actively promoting innovative thinking, practice, and policymaking. Some

of the NITI Aayog's accomplishments under his leadership include:

- Formulating many significant innovative policies since its founding on January 1, 2015
- Establishing "Team Hub" as a cooperative working platform between Centre & States
- Promoting healthy competition among developing states and regional councils
- Creating "The Knowledge and Innovation Hub" to extend think tank capabilities
- Founding an innovation platform to bring fresh ideas to the government
- Forming an innovation ecosystem through the Atal Innovation Mission to promote growth
- Establishing more than 7,500 Atal Tinkering Labs in schools with a target of 50,000 by 2030
- Setting up 67 Atal Community Incubation Centres to encourage start-ups for young innovators
- Developing a common platform to capture new ideas from industry, academia, and society
- Cutting across silos to reduce malnourishment through the Poshaan Abhiyan program
- Instilling accountability through outcome-based monitoring in real time
- Promoting a spirit of competitive federalism across key verticals
- Instituting short response time for business tenders

In receiving this award, Dr. Kumar is following other prestigious leaders in innovation, such as the Honorable Pranab Mukherjee, former President of India, and John Chambers, former chairman of Cisco. In his introductory speech, Dr. Iyer emphasized the value of innovation that the NITI Aayog has fostered across corporations, academia, and the government to truly address fundamental challenges. He expressed Berkeley's commitment to partnering with the NITI Aayog as they work to expand India's research initiatives associated with sustainable business models to support the goal of transforming India. Dr. Iyer looked forward to the ongoing collaboration between the NITI Aayog and Berkeley as a great platform contributing to India's growth and successes.

Acceptance Speech & Keynote
On behalf of the NITI Aayog, Dr. Kumar expressed his gratitude for receiving the award. He thanked UC Berkeley for recognizing the organization's efforts in creating an innovation ecosystem and trust between the government and the corporate sector in India. The NITI Aayog continues to strive as much as possible in these efforts, and he said that this award would encourage them to constantly improve and create more impact.

Founded in 2015, the NITI Aayog replaced the Planning Commission of India and took charge of central planning in India with the commitment to work with and support private investors and entrepreneurship. The NITI Aayog is the think tank of the country and connects it with the world outside to gain ideas which can be useful for policy making. The NITI Aayog increasingly puts efforts into developing blueprints for individual states in the country by recognizing that each state is a unique entity requiring specific development. The aim is to create good policy making instead of competitive populism among the states, and this entails cooperation with the private sector as the only way forward for India. In this respect, Dr. Kumar looks forward to the cooperation with UC Berkeley which began in 2021 as part of a five-year MoU. Leveraging the power of the corporate sector in the process of building talent is a key element for India's future. He encouraged all the participants at the Berkeley Innovation Forum to tell the government how to make this relationship between Berkeley, the premium university of the world, and the NITI Aayog, the premium think tank in India, useful for India's corporations and entrepreneurs. He is looking forward to the ideas and practical recommendations coming out of this forum.

He applauded the rebuilding initiative with its relevant, well-designed segments that align with the NITI Aayog's efforts. Making India a global manufacturing hub will reinforce India's first-ever active industry policy that clearly identifies 14 sectors for expansion to reach a global scale and global competitiveness. Dr. Kumar emphasized that the NITI Aayog stands for a self-reliant India, not a self-sufficient India, that engages more with the rest of the world on a competitive basis. India wants to be a truly open economy to become a better partner for global trade, finance, and technology. All incentives from policies target these ambitions – such as quadrupling India's global export share in the next decade to be a reliant partner while making the transition toward a middle-income economy.

Regarding the acceleration of skill development, India has blossomed in recent years. There were about 3,000 startups in the country in 2012, and as of January 2022 the number had increased to 61,000. Those represent huge potential, and Dr. Kumar hoped that the Berkeley Initiative would work with these startups and help them to become commercially viable, financially sustainable, and globally competitive. The NITI Aayog has already established 9,500 Atel innovation mission labs in secondary schools, and they are committed to establishing a total of 50,000 to dramatically change the education system. The program is designed to encourage young talent to become familiar with the latest technology and pursue entrepreneurial activities. Dr. Kumar encourages corporations to leverage and cooperate with such talent.

Dr. Kumar emphasized India's ambitious focus on technology sectors, such as 5G connectivity, space economy, biotechnology, green energy, and clean mobility. These areas mean a new paradigm for India: It is not about wanting to be in areas where India can't compete with the rest of the world, but about actively shaping key technology sectors as the foundation for strong, future growth and development of India's economy and society. UC Berkeley could serve as a strong partner to realize India's vision and mission.

Transforming these ambitions into successful outcomes can only happen if trust between the government and the corporate sector is created as a foundation for innovation. This will require a mindset shift on both sides, as this trust is not present to the extent that it should be. Dr. Kumar emphasized that building the basis of trust needs to be at the core of the Rebuilding India Initiative and solicited recommendations for how to do it.

The year 2047 will mark the 100-year celebration of India's independence. It remains open what India's vision and mission for this date will be. Personally, Dr. Kumar expects that India will be the third-largest economy in the world. However, it will require alignment between ethics, environment, and morals to create trust between industry and government. This can be a big chance for India to develop its own model. Not having completed the economic transition provides India with unique opportunities to integrate the environment into its growth and development. India's equity needs to be ensured through green and economic alignment. Harnessing frontline technologies from multiple sectors acts as a catalyzer for becoming a bright role model for achieving economic growth compatible with our environment.

Dr. Kumar concluded that civil society, government, corporates, and academia need to work together to achieve India's strong ambitions with India's unique model, and suggested that any rec-ommendations on India's vision and how to establish trust across all stakeholders would be very welcome.

KEYNOTE REMARKS ON DIGITAL TRANSFORMATION

The CTO of a European telecommunications company delivered a speech on digital transformation. He explained that, in 1990, only 5 million mobile subscriptions existed in India. This showed that the country was tremendously lagging behind developed econo-mies. Now, a staggering 80.5% mobile penetration in India shows how many advancements there have been on the road from 2G to 5G. In his keynote remarks, the CTO of a European telecommu-nications company emphasized the expectational opportunities coming with 5G. An enormous amount of bandwidth and mas-sive connections at the same time allow not only connectivity on a whole new level for end users but also the power to accelerate developments in the industry of things, edge computing, smart home, smart farming, and healthcare among other sectors.

The 5G standard is becoming an open innovation platform where many actors can plug in and innovate. The speaker shared his excitement for new possibilities and his work with BIFI (the Berkeley Innovation Forum India) to explore how 5G can unlock its full potential with new use cases, strengthening initiatives for manufacturing, education, and last-mile connectivity. 5G can leap-frog current progress in green and sustainable innovation, digi-tal education, healthcare, and smart supply chains. His company is developing a strong scope in India, both in urban and rural sectors.

TABLE DISCUSSION FOR INITIATIVE #1: MAKING INDIA A GLOBAL MANUFACTURING HUB

Discussing how to lift India's manufacturing sector, the COO of an Indian conglomerate emphasized the following points which he gained from discussions with industry and government executives:

- Creating a seamless and smooth link between academia and industry. There is still a serious shortage of available in-house technologies for many products, which is an impediment for further growth. While close ties between academia and industry are prevalent in the U.S., India lacks such relationships. The government can be a facilitator to expand fruitful exchange.
- Introducing new intellectual inputs into the industry. There is a serious challenge in designing high-value products, or even lower-value ones such as a mouse. Design is missing and Indian manufacturing is often associated with putting compounds together instead of inventing machines/products and then producing at scale.
- Designing ecosystem cluster approaches for different industries where many smaller players can co-exist. That helps with just-in-time approaches, reduced supply chain cost, better efficiency, and synergy effects to push manufacturing growth.
- Improving the availability of skilled labor. Large companies tend to have their own infrastructure and talent pipeline. However, it is a challenge to get the right amount of labor at the place where the industry needs it.
- Improving the cost structure. Having world-beating cost structures in place is not just a requirement for the above-mentioned points, but also the key success factor in making India

the factory of the world. Being better than China demands achieving industry growth objectives at the right costs.

- Having a single-window clearance system for approvals in place. Setting up factories and running businesses comes with a plethora of regulations and requirements that vary across states while additionally running into central regulations. To improve the ease of doing business, all the requirements should be made transparent and available on a portal where people can learn how to obtain the necessary clearances and comply with the regulations.
- Improving the infrastructure for supply chains within the country. Road, port, and water infrastructure need to be improved at a very rapid pace. Also, the approach needs to overcome scatteredness where, for example, a port is world-class but the roads leading from it are not sufficiently developed to allow for fast and cost-competitive movement of goods.
- Establishing a framework for improved angel investing in the manufacturing sector. Policies that provide incentives such as tax breaks to stimulate entrepreneurship and R&D are needed.
- Standardizing rules across states for moving products and services.

Table Recommendations

The panel began by discussing how to increase India's IP creation instead of relying on foreign companies for manufacturing and how to increase export share. These were their recommendations:

Policy Making

- Improve perception and rank of the ease of doing business in India to increase foreign direct investment (FDI).

- Change Make in India Incentive from short-term to long-term. Because of the lack of an industry ecosystem, the objective of Make in India reaching a global scale and becoming a self-sufficient manufacturer is not feasible.
- Address the gap between policy making and policy execution. Local and state bodies often don't have the capabilities to implement policies or execute policies differently from how they were originally designed.
- Ease access and decrease fees to participate in the PLI (production-linked incentive) schemes set out by the National Investment Promotion & Facilitation Agency.
- Establish a lean policy for land, labor, and funds as a complete process to enable efficient and effective scale-up of manufacturing in India. This can enable small manufacturing, evolving toward a robust framework for quick growth.

R&D Investment & Growth Strategy

- Increase renewable energy production. Almost 80% of energy is being imported, putting pressure on energy prices. Renewable energy needs to take a larger share of the energy mix to decrease energy costs. Local government restrictions slow down progress.
- Improve backward integration of critical materials. Importing critical materials creates a big risk of volatile prices which lead to inflation.
- Invest in forthcoming technology that can make India the hydrogen hub of the world. Ambitions should come with responsible objectives. 70% of the power produced in India is currently through Siemens technology (Germany). India can invest in its own IP within the renewable energy sector to export technology rather than import it.

- Apply success factors and trust factors from the service industry to the manufacturing sector. 9 out of 10 Indian "unicorns" are in the service sector, reflecting a huge lack of product-based innovation and manufacturing. The ease of doing business needs to be improved for land, labor laws, and business clearance. Reforms need to come quickly.
- Ensure that products manufactured in India are eligible for global export.
- Improve investment in original design and R&D to shift Indian manufacturing from assembly of foreign components to original equipment and component manufacturing. Ensure that components such as chips are manufactured in India, leading bigger players to come to India because of the low cost and local availability of technology components (as compared to China).

Ecosystem Strategy

- Build a level of trust that can be executed across the different levels and entities. Global businesses face trust issues when, despite their international success, they need to prove their business model and technology to the government. Trust issues are not as obvious as labor shortages or infrastructure, making this a very subjective, elusive goal. Identifying common ground and clarity in communication are key factors to increase trust.
- The economy design needs to shift from local to global scaling. Infrastructure and manufacturing upscaling need to go hand in hand with geopolitical strategic positioning to ensure demand from global markets. Established private players in India need to align with a global growth strategy to ensure supply.

- Create the next generation of industry, technologies, and workforce rather than replicating the existing models.
- Have a uniform segregated strategy for manufacturing. Create geographical and demographic-based clusters that leverage unique strengths to become successful, specialized industry clusters. Labor, capital, and land gap analysis can map out locations and solve micro problems.

TABLE DISCUSSION FOR INITIATIVE #2: SKILL DEVELOPMENT

The managing director of the South Asian branch of an American software company opened this discussion by remarking that education is a topic near to everyone's heart. Every innovation in education springs from technology, and new thinking leads to new business models and new consumer behavior. The last-mile connectivity through digital technology is therefore a foundation for innovative education today.

We are at a stage in our lives where we face both a challenging array of needs and an enormous convergence of technology. There are three overlapping situations which are relevant here:

- The last big revolution that connected humans was the internet. Although only half of the world is connected to the internet, it has created a $150 trillion dollar economy. Humans need to be connected to each other, but connections must also be built between humans and objects, and different types of objects must be linked to each other as well. This creates a new internet – a more personalized internet that could be worth 10 times what it is today.

- India is at the stage of readiness for such a new digital revolution. The question is how 600 million Indian youth can step into this new world where technology converges to disrupt business models and, more importantly, the economy. India is a very unique nation, and because resources are scarce its people have learned to be competitive within limitations. India knows that despite scarce resources it will continue to do well, especially in academia. Every year, one million STEM students come to the marketplace and 61K technology-oriented startups are launched. With 6 to 7 million developers, India is one of the largest resources for IT. Combining this power brings the opportunity for India to become the garage of the world.
- Understanding how to apply cutting-edge technology to India's needs requires leadership – top-down leadership to address a few grand challenges that will inspire the many to apply it in smaller formats. Education, healthcare, agriculture, and language barriers are all challenges that can be addressed through technology. 5G and 6G are becoming affordable options to reach the last mile. There is an opportunity to let India become the back office of the world by increasingly leveraging artificial intelligence, increasing productivity and value creation.

The question is how to apply these use cases and vast technological developments to education. In India, the "good enough" students have generally been encouraged to take science and the "not good enough" students to take arts. However, the applicability of education and building the intersection of art and science are crucial today, as both disciplines are important. There needs to be trust on various sides to convert objectives, missions, or requirements into an understanding of the scope of work. If that comes with leadership, it forms a foundation that becomes a vehicle for action.

This discussion was co-chaired by a government official who plays a key role in setting India's educational policies. He emphasized the government's work in addressing access, quality education, affordability, and partner accountability as important aspects to transform and empower the educational system. There are concerns, especially from parents, that education investment needs to translate into employment. To achieve this goal, there are many aspects to consider:

- There should be relevant, dynamic curricula and different skill sets for problem-solving, R&D, and entrepreneurship.
- Engagement with the industry is essential for academic curricula development, and the training of faculty is equally important as training the students.
- Students should be exposed to industry through internships.
- Education should be sustainable. The central government should provide basic architecture while industry, academia, and government bodies test and launch innovative educational programs such as online education and digital universities with a focus on relevant skills sought by industry.
- All Indian languages should be integrated to tap into the full potential of innovation from the country's vast diversity. The government is focused on developing the last mile, language translation, and providing people with education in their mother tongue alongside English.
- Ease of doing business needs to be applied to education to minimize the complexity of regulations while ensuring trust through robust systems.
- Policymaking needs to translate into execution in collaboration with the industry and academia to gain speed and scale to address challenges quickly and comprehensively.

Table Recommendations

Policy Making

- Enable universally recognized micro-credentialing for skills that meet commercial needs. Unlocking human capital helps upskilling and entering the workforce more quickly. Universal micro-credential standardization is needed, as many companies use different systems. IACT could be the vehicle to drive this standardization recognition process to create a strong database of proven talent (credit bank) under the E4 objective (education, employability, employment, entrepreneurship) while minimizing fudging. All stakeholders need to talk together.
- Change the student testing paradigm. Education should be for skills, not for a degree to build capability for jobs and create value. Industry and the government need to come together and ensure the implementation.

Ecosystem Strategy

- Identify an action plan and points. Addressing the educational challenges requires an understanding of how all the companies can contribute to curriculum development and come up with an action plan.
- Have robust success metrics for action plans in place. What does education mean in India? What is a new definition of the curriculum? What is required to make "educated in India" a global brand for excellence?
- Digital platforms need to become more comprehensive. Most digital learning platforms are not scalable because the use cases are very specific but not consolidated. Open Innovation can be used to create a GitHub for education

that allows flexible upskilling and reskilling, providing equal opportunities and democratizing education.

- Encourage students to question the status quo. Creating opportunities to disrupt outdated thinking is needed within the current education system in India.
- Skill focus needs to go beyond just digital skills. The manufacturing sector demands technicians, engineers, and workmen, and therefore skills training needs to be developed to meet broad industry needs.

Development & Execution Strategy

- Implementation feasibility is critical. Educating and training 600 million young people is a big goal and cannot be done through a one-size-fits-all solution. Maybe the education system needs to be tiered, with local hubs catering to specialized training needs to get more people into the educational system.
- Employability needs to increase. Currently, 50% of people who graduate college are not employable. India needs holistic education and a redefinition of relevant skill sets, including creativity and communication.
- Ensure scalability. Companies conduct many pilots that are not being scaled. A strong pull needs to be created so that the industry moves toward scale. The country needs to scale up a hundredfold compared to its current situation.
- Industry hiring for skills rather than degrees is a new paradigm, but still not the norm.
- Entrepreneurship is in the Indian DNA but is mainly unleashed abroad.
- Create multiple studies on the educational system, gather the statistics, and present the architecture on how to move the initiative forward.

- Improve foundational skills, as 82% of students lack them. India is second-last in PISA scores. Start from scratch to improve the foundational skills and grow them further.

TABLE DISCUSSION FOR INITIATIVE #3: LAST-MILE CONNECTIVITY

The premise of last-mile connectivity is that we explore digital connectivity, which serves as the main success driver for inclusive growth and offers vast potential for innovation. Connectivity is fundamental to unleashing potential, especially at the bottom of the pyramid, which could allow stakeholders to tap into a $3 trillion opportunity. Logistics and market linkages are benefits that create new value. Most importantly, new human benefits arise when people are mobilized and communities are formed through connectivity. Thus, the exploration of digital connectivity needs to focus on three dimensions: digital, physical, and human connectivity.

In order to unleash the full potential of technology, the challenges in building use cases related to connectivity need to be addressed, and so do the challenges in building the connectivity itself. In this discussion, the president of an Indian telecommunications company laid out three success factors in overcoming these challenges:

- Affordability. Reaching the bottom of the pyramid can only succeed when people can afford to connect.
- Goal alignment. When connectivity is being built, local communities and companies might have different goals. Ease of doing business and one-stop clearances from the government alongside affordable charges from the corporate side

can minimize those hurdles. Support is especially needed in areas where there are low margins. Rollout of last-mile connectivity needs to be done in a mission mode, where local, central government, and providers are talking to one another to avoid misalignment.

- Resources. Capital (private and public) is required to scale last-mile connectivity across the country in time and quality.
- There are numerous use cases that are leveraging last-mile connectivity. With the onset of the COVID-19 pandemic, applications for digital connectivity dramatically increased. In healthcare, telemedicine played a special role in reaching patients, while in education digital connectivity has been the link between teachers and students.
- From the Smart Village Movement pilot, we've learned that there needs to be value creation and capture. Gramin Healthcare created value through 24/7 remote healthcare while capturing value through pharmacy sales instead of telemedicine sales. The Open Innovation approach can be an important driver for connectivity to link different entities into one business model while providing mutual benefits.
- Learning from healthcare, requirements for successful use cases can be identified:
- Educating people who will be supplying or serving recipients through digital means.
- Broad education about digital connectivity is required to accelerate other use cases, such as in education, agriculture, and logistics. The mainstream economy can add value when digital connectivity is fully integrated to unlock new growth potential.
- An Indian government official concluded this presentation by emphasizing the need for a mission mode. In his state, access to tap water in every house increased from 3%

to 30% in three years thanks to an aligned mission mode shared by all stakeholders responsible for the outcome. A policy recommendation through the NITI Aayog to make digital connectivity available for every household could accelerate this initiative into a mission rather than a decentralized local program.

Table Recommendations

Policy Making

- Create reformative systems for policies. Policies should allow easy investment in stakeholders to keep digital connections alive (e.g., health insurance in remote areas backed by digital solutions). This would give incentives to many stakeholders to foster growth; CSR funds could be invested through this.
- Create an infrastructure map and make it available to the private and public sector to find and link communities, industries, and governments. This would help form policies, create alignment, and unlock new, scalable innovations.
- Government should enable the creation of infrastructure through various goal-aligned partners in the private sector rather than building itself.

Ecosystem Strategy

- There could be a centralized infrastructure for communication in a village or set of villages. These hubs could also further business activities.
- Every Indian could be onboarded to the digital world quite easily and quickly. However, this needs to be done in a mission mode across the central, state, and local governments,

as well as operator and consumer groups. Once they are all part of one mission, it can be achieved.

- The initiative should be addressed from both the supply and demand perspectives. Supply issue: infrastructure needs to be built and aligned. Demand issue: availability, affordability, accessibility, applicability (education, booking, trade, etc.).
- Models to develop viable use cases should be enabled and supported. Corporate digital platforms could be leveraged to create replicable model villages.
- All efforts and initiatives need to be defined with specific metrics. What is the impact? Is everyone benefiting from the initiative? If you don't deliver content to the people, how can they benefit? If they don't see any benefit, they won't use it. Relevant KPIs need to be developed.

Implementation Strategy

- More than 90% of the total cost for laying fiber goes to the local government bodies, as seen in smaller cities. This is a major barrier to cost-efficient scaling of digital connectivity. Alignment is required to ensure benefits for the government and the operators while avoiding high costs. The 2018 telegraph rules asked states to adopt central government regulations that made the process more expensive. The rules have to be further tightened so that additional costs are not added. This should be done through parliament rather than local government
- To accelerate traction and consumer adoption, access could be granted as a fundamental right (for free) while consumption charges could pay back investment later.
- Bandwidth and quality need to be increased. Even in digital connection, there might be severe language barriers

and digital literacy issues. Meeting those needs is important; the moment bandwidth is improved, language issues can be eradicated through AI.

- Resources like spectrum and capital need to be increased, given India's immense size and population.
- Smartphone penetration should be increased through affordable devices, enabling the internet to come to all corners of India and change how people interact and conduct business.
- Use cases need to be applicable and create value for the individual and society.
- There needs to be dynamic content as required by vast-changing technologies and surroundings.

Further Discussion

The invited government officers and heads of elite firms were asked to reconvene in their appointed groups per initiative to further develop their recommendations on how to take the Rebuilding India Initiatives forward. Discussions on Day 2 focused on finalizing action plans for each initiative and presenting them to Dr. Rajiv Kumar.

Welcome from The NITI Aayog

Manglesh Yadav, director of the NITI Aayog's Atal Innovation Mission, welcomed the Forum on Day 2 and expressed the value of the collaboration with UC Berkeley and all the participating corporations across industries. The NITI Aayog is the nodal think tank of India for design policy, program framework, monitoring, and evaluation of cooperative federalism. Key initiatives include:

- Working with all of India's states
- Transforming policy environment

- Monitoring and evaluation
- Fostering knowledge and innovation
- COVID-19 response
- The goal of the Atal Innovation Mission is to create an ecosystem that can grow and catch up with innovation across the world, driving problem-driven solutions through multiple stakeholders:
- Atal Tinkering Labs to foster an innovative mindset in schools
- Atal Incubation Centers to foster startups (2,800 have been supported so far)
- Atal New India Challenges to foster product innovation
- Atal Community Innovation Centers
- ANC-Arise to foster MSME
- The innovation value chain includes researching problems, supporting and advising startups, helping pilot ideas, and making large-scale deployments with direct grant funding of up to 50 crores.

Success Stories:

- Youth Collab: Program to support social entrepreneurs to let them access markets. Four cohorts were run to provide entrepreneurs with guidance and capacity training for five months, with a final presentation from the top three startups pitching to social impact investors and officials.
- Adobe is a corporate partner for launching marketable products. Challenges attract students who apply with a proposal for a solution. Short-listed ideas get mentor support and guidance. Ready-made solutions are shared with stakeholders in industry. 85 IPs have been created and eight startups have reached the market so far.

- Linking startups and R&D with industry. Industry can come with an innovation requirement or respond to innovation available within the NITI Aayog ecosystem. Examples:
  - o IKEA approached the NITI Aayog regarding water challenges and was provided with a repository of innovative startups. Partnerships were then facilitated by the NITI Aayog.
  - o The Bill and Melinda Gates Foundation sought innovative ideas and processes to produce face masks and tests during COVID. The NITI Aayog facilitated innovation sprints by academia, industry, and the government.

DATA PRESENTATION FROM THE 2022 BERKELEY INNOVATION FORUM INDIA SURVEY

At the beginning of the conference, a survey was handed out to all participants asking about their priorities regarding relevant challenges and needs for their business success (n=30). This was done before the working sessions began to minimize the probability of data bias. The survey ranked challenges in terms of priority and importance for business success.

Professor Darwin discussed the results in this presentation:

1. Talent acquisition has the biggest priority while last-mile connection challenges remain the biggest bottleneck to business growth.

Although last-mile connectivity is the biggest factor impacting business success, talent acquisition remains the top-ranked priority. Participating companies emphasized that they struggle with continuously filling their talent pipeline in India. Multinationals' global structure allows them to address short-term talent gaps by sourcing from abroad. This aspect helps them deal better with talent shortages compared with SMEs, which have neither the brand to compete with prestigious companies nor the global embeddedness to source from abroad. This puts additional pressure to win talent and strengthen SMEs in India.

In both priority and weight, last-mile connectivity is perceived as a bigger challenge than acquiring and retaining customers. Without sufficient connectivity, there is an enormous barrier to reaching the more underserved audiences, putting pressure on domestic growth. At the same time, target groups that don't have access to digital products and services miss out on their own potential to develop toward a middle-income level.

Supply chain issues remain high in priority and importance, reflecting the aftermath of COVID-19, chip shortages, and geopolitical uncertainty. Interestingly, public infrastructure seems to have a low impact on business success compared to service provider issues. This reflects the large share of service-based businesses compared to product-based businesses represented at this conference and across India in general. For example, 9 out of 10 unicorns in India are service-based businesses. Only one is based on product development, manufacturing, and sales, requiring traditional heavy infrastructure investment in things like roads, ports, and railroads.

2. The inflow of knowledge remains a high priority, while opening up to form viable collaborations (outflow) has the biggest impact on business.

The sourcing of knowledge, expertise, and IP into large organizations has been a proven strategy for remaining innovative.

Ideas and expertise that are not available in-house complement the infrastructure, scale, and resources a large company has to offer.

In his 2003 book *Open Innovation: The New Imperative for Creating and Profiting from Technology*, Henry Chesbrough defined Open Innovation as "the use of purposive inflows and outflows of knowledge to accelerate internal innovation, and expand the markets for external use of innovation, respectively." Since then, the sourcing of external knowledge has become an integral part of large companies' innovation and business development strategy.

To form meaningful and long-term collaborations with other companies, businesses also need to open up their knowledge bases to create mutual benefits for all ecosystem members. We can see that knowledge outflow for collaboration has the biggest impact on business success, emphasizing the need to create win-win situations among partners.

3. Ecosystem alignment issues have both the highest priority and importance for businesses.

Ecosystems that don't align with their vision, mission, and action plans are insufficient to create and absorb value. This is the challenge that participants face the most. Government incentives and infrastructure availability can foster the creation of industry cluster ecosystems. However, it takes the triple helix of industry, academia, and government to jointly align for developing strong ecosystems and overcoming ecosystem formation challenges. This data confirms that India needs to create strong alignment across those stakeholders as the underlying fabric to let ecosystems thrive.

4. Dynamic capabilities are the skills needed going forward while imitability issues affect businesses the most.

In their 1997 research paper "Dynamic Capabilities and Strategic Management," David Teece, Gary Pisano, and Amy Shuen discussed how a company can display dynamic capabilities. To do so, it must effectively react to rapidly changing environments by integrating, building, and reconfiguring internal and external competencies, and also lead with a vision that forms new business models, integrating a dynamic approach for increasing resiliency while opening and shaping new growth avenues.

The ability to effectively orchestrate people, assets, and resources breaks with the predominant strategy of only orchestrating assets that are on one's balance sheet. Participants understand that such leadership abilities are the requirement of the hour, given our highly dynamic markets, innovation landscape, and geopolitics. They rank dynamic capabilities as their first priority for leadership. However, in terms of business impact, respondents emphasize that protecting there is the most important factor.

5. Consistency in policies is sought the most.

To make the triple-helix structure work, government support needs to be consistent and transparent. Participants emphasize that a stable political environment helps them with investment projects that have large project horizons. If policies change and formerly promised subsidies alter, projects might face a huge overhead and run out of the original budget. Planning security through public policy consistency and industry-friendly applicability reflects another instrumental success factor for accelerating the discussed initiatives.

Action Plan for Initiative #2: Education as Fabric for All Initiatives

Introducing the next topic, the lead scientist of an American governmental organization emphasized education as an underlying theme for all initiatives to have better-trained labor on both technical and soft skills. This requires:

- Housing all corporate training programs under one roof (GitHub Open Access)
- Agnostic facilitators to evaluate and curate submitted content based on educational needs (UC Berkeley could do this)
- Dissemination of content to local communities through the creation of innovation hubs throughout the country
- Tiered approach of a hub to serve the communities most in need
- Mentor and peer-to-peer approaches to guide use of content and career counseling.

To prepare for this program, a six-month study group should be formed to identify demand and supply. Critical to success for the dissemination of information is the integration as a complementary offering within the existing curriculum. Innovation hubs can facilitate onboarding and facilitation. These hubs can be established both virtually and physically, such as in local schools. Community solutions are needed to address the needs of local people. The process can be accelerated by identifying existing hubs where innovation has already reached a certain level. A playbook could reveal the existing gaps and potential. Global benchmarking is the baseline. Connecting the dots is important to identify and integrate larger scales. Tapping into the maximum potential is also vital, given the fact that the head of the family is often the only one with access to the internet.

Table Recommendations:

- Internet providers need to come forward to ensure internet availability and facility. Often, the right specs and hardware are missing. A plan that includes short-, mid-, and long-term solutions is needed.
- There can be digital spaces within Gram Panjab to utilize the existing available infrastructure.
- Penetration of digital education raises the question of gender equality that needs to be addressed.
- Marrying the needs of industry and program audiences can create equilibrium between demand for and supply of jobs. However, industry cannot be the only offering because many other skills, such as carpentry, are in demand.
- Industry offices should work directly with schools and online hubs to identify skill-fit through aggregation techniques. Asset mapping can ensure that the needs of communities are being addressed by both the government and industry. Companies must commit to partnerships through a central program as opposed to various separate partnerships on an individual corporate level.

FINAL PRESENTATIONS TO DR. RAJIV KUMAR

Final Presentation #1: Making India a Global Manufacturing Hub

This presentation was chaired by the COO of an Indian conglomerate, with contributions from more than thirty tech industry executives from India, Europe, and America. They offered the following objectives aimed at moving India to the forefront of global manufacturing:

Improve cost competitiveness position of India's manufacturing

- Win-Win Academia-Industry Collaboration
  o Create state of art technology/design
  o Have best-in-class products
  o Minimize capital expenditures and operating expenses
- Energy cost management
  o Accelerate renewable energy growth
  o Let industry benefit from low-cost energy production
  o Reduce cross-substitution for industry
- Supply chain cost reduction
  o Expand Gatishakti mission
  o Scale multimodal movement of goods through rail and coastal transport rather than by road
- Angel investing in manufacturing by the government
  o Initiate new R&D
  o Sustain and scale early-stage innovation
- Regulations
  o Simplify and reduce regulations to minimize affiliated regulatory costs for industry

Simplify governance and improve ease of doing business

- Simpler and stable policy framework
  o Reduce frequent changes in taxation and other policies
  o Minimize overhead costs for businesses and manufacturing plants caused by changing frameworks
  o Single window time-bound clearance system
- Minimize rules and clearances to establish manufacturing facilities
  o Avoid ambiguity regarding requirements
  o Improve compliance planning to avoid last-minute delays and costs for large projects.

- Simplify labor laws
  - o Reduce over-governance and avoid demotivation of entrepreneurs as they start manufacturing
- Decriminalize and reduce the compliance burden
  - o Avoid treating minor errors as criminal offenses
  - o Provide a stable and fair system to attract investors

Develop clusters of manufacturing as sunrise sectors through ecosystems

- Provide a platform where suppliers co-exist, unlocking synergy effects and attractiveness for new investors
- Unlock new growth by improving both domestic and export markets
- Foster sustainable and cutting-edge technology
- Facilitate cost-competitiveness and product quality
- Create incentives to make investors and industry join sunrise clusters

What can we achieve with these actions?

- Rapid growth of manufacturing
- Factory of the world
- Jobs
- Multiplier effect on other sectors
- Improved trade balance
- Tax collections/government revenue

Response from Dr. Kumar

India has been very weak at product innovation so far. Owners of industries need to facilitate increased innovation activities to launch best-in-class products. Academia and industry collaboration can help achieve this, using innovation to become cost competitive. Dr. Kumar proposed that the next forum could talk about how to achieve product innovation in India through collaboration and open innovation.

The acceleration of renewable energy is important, and the government is in the process of facilitating India's growth. Dr. Kumar suggested that industry could install solar and wind parks off-grid, as the costs can be lower than getting energy from the grid while earning extra money by selling energy surplus back into the grid.

Angel investing is being done by Atal Innovation Mission, and the idea of initial equity investment into startups is being discussed and will soon be implemented.

There are many approvals needed, and the prime minister has been raising this issue. The NITI Aayog is working on simplifying and reducing compliance for industry. Some requirements are under-publicized and may arise unexpectedly. Dr. Kumar raised the following questions that were addressed in a follow-up meeting in May 2022:

- What are the most important compliance/approval issues?
- How can successful industry clusters be established in India?

QUESTIONS FOR THE INDUSTRY – ADDRESSED AT THE FOLLOW-UP MEETING

1st **Question:** What are the most important compliance/approval issues?

From the CEO of an Indian chemical corporation:

- Regulations differ across company-specific variables:
  o *Industry:* There are different regulations under different ministries responsible for different categories. It takes a lot of time to navigate through this landscape and also wastes government resources (addressing the needs of the companies and helping them find the right process). Standardization across industry categories is needed.
  o *New vs old companies:* New industries start with new rules while established companies have different ones. New rules should be applicable to old ones as well.
- Time to get permissions halts projects. The lack of permissions to roll out new high-capital intensive projects often delays schedules, causing overall time overruns of 15%.
- Land use compliance. Many permissions are needed. The process can be sped up through the state governments.
- Labor law compliance. Companies are held overly responsible for everything their employees do. This creates not only costly issues for the companies but also a system of mistrust. The trust in corporations doing it right needs to improve.
- Suggestions:
- There need to be better and larger incentives for companies to reduce their GHG emissions.
- Companies that are compliant with regulations should get a status that makes them eligible for rapid expansion support to further grow business in a lean, less bureaucratic way.
- From an executive of the Indian branch of an international beverage company:
- My company interacts with state governments, and the collaboration varies drastically across different states. The compliance side is getting better, but issues remain:

- Implementation of online approval is offline. Online approval is hybrid rather than digital. Physical documents need to be sent to ministries that take a lot of time to process them manually. This hybrid approach creates costs for both companies and the government.
- Pollution Compliance varies between central and state. My company has 15 factories in India. Compliance is sent to state and central pollution control boards that are not in line with each other and have different expectations.
- States have different industrial policies. To speed up manufacturing, the NITI Aayog should influence industrial policies by providing companies with more incentives for green production and women's employment. It is important to push those agendas.
- From the chairman of an Indian electronics company:
- Suggestions for improving industrial policies and compliance framework with a focus on manufacturing:
- Cost disadvantage through missing subsidies. There are high-cost disadvantages in logistics because of the absence of subsidies compared to China and Vietnam, where these subsidies contributed to cost reductions of 1% and 0.5%, respectively, as of 2019.
- High costs of capital required for production activities. Mobile phone manufacturing is highly capital- and technology-intensive because it requires the latest high-volume machinery, thereby necessitating huge investments. An increase in tariffs/BCD on imports of P&C also risks increasing the cost of final products. A continuous rise in BCD is proposed wherever subsidies cannot be granted, but tariffs also do not guarantee more revenue generation.
- Weak IP rights regime. IP base is not strong enough in terms of development and facilitation as well as protection

of rights. Low subsidies on patent costs affect innovations in India.

2nd Question: How can successful industry clusters be established in India?

From the chairman of an Indian electronics company:

- Continuation of the PLI scheme. In absence of radical tariffs, tax and investment climate reforms, India will have to continue to provide some form of incentives to make it an attractive destination for manufacturing. Furthermore, the scope of PLI needs to be extended to all consumer electronics and their components, similar to the mobile phones and IT hardware policies.
- Decrease high import dependence, mainly on China, particularly during COVID-19. Evidence exists for Q2 2020 that a few Chinese firms located in India, including Xiaomi and Oppo, imported smartphones from China because of issues with increasing production in Indian factories to meet high demand. India's restriction on Chinese imports during May-June 2020 also delayed production by OEMs in India because of a lack of stock of materials and inputs. Smartphone manufacturers (including the ones working under PLI) are highly dependent on China for components and related equipment.

From the CEO of the Indian branch of a multinational tech company:

My company was the only IT player selected for the PLI scheme. We met our one-year target for local computer manufacturing in

Chennai, and the server line is being expanded. Learning from the PLI, there are challenges that need to be addressed to unlock more potential and attract new players:

- Increase incentives that are linked to PLI. Currently, the subsidy is not sufficient to become cost competitive. An increase of 2-3% could vastly improve cost-competitiveness.
- Increase the time frame of the PLI.
- From the CEO of an Indian management consulting firm:
- Start, scale, and sustain manufacturing. Industrial policy can best succeed in a pro-trade and pro-market environment. India should try to reap the maximum benefits from existing global players (GVCs) and from its current free trade agreements, and also explore new trade partners to scale up assembly activities.
- Local mapping of resources throughout the country. The lack of a database for Indian electronics production (value and volume terms) at a disaggregated level is a major limitation for undertaking credible analysis. State and central governments could better align with data availability regarding land, labor, and finance. Specific zones can be identified to help create industry clusters, while policy work can improve with specific, localized policies where resources can be made more accessible.

Final Presentation #2: Skilling 600 Million Youth

This presentation was co-chaired by the managing director of the South Asian branch of an American software company and an Indian state government official, with contributions from nearly 20 tech industry executives. They offered the following thoughts on building a pool of skilled technological workers in India:

Talent & Skill Development Through Digital Platforms

- House all corporate training programs under one roof
  - o Example: Github Open Access
- Find a facilitator to evaluate and curate submitted content
  - o UC Berkeley could be an ideal non-agnostic facilitator, and could use data for research and student projects
- Disseminate content to local communities through the creation of innovation hubs throughout the country.
  - o A tiered approach should exist to serve the communities most in need (rural villages, third-tier cities to first-tier cities)
  - o Mentor and peer-to-peer approach will guide the use of content, career counseling, etc.

Critical Success Factors

- Appoint POC for nodal education and skilling to integrate multiple stakeholders. Many programs exist across ministries and departments, making it difficult for the industry to find the right fit for initiating private-public partnerships. Addressing this situation will help to optimize resources.
- Leverage and aggregate ongoing ecosystem initiatives (platform, content, digital tools, skilling of teachers) such as Samshiksha. There are a plethora of private players and educational institutions in the education field. One ecosystem that facilitates communication, student mobility, and industry exchange can unlock network effects to create a win-win situation for all stakeholders.
- Employ an agnostic body for benchmarking of outcomes and impact. Establishing certain metrics to evaluate the success of any educational program helps in targeting investments into scaling efforts.

- Request government support in scaling impactful programs based on metrics. There are many pilots in education that can create impact and benefit, but industry is not able to move beyond a handful of universities and a few thousand students. There is considerable demand for further, speedy scaling, and government support is needed because the educational system is complex, scattered, and highly regulated.
- Adopt flexibility and agility in credentialing and credits. Currently, students have a formalized education system and degrees. They also have many opportunities outside classrooms to follow their interests and upskill themselves. Flexibility on how credentials and certifications can be recognized is needed, as employers' demand for skills is constantly changing. This would further fuel the democratization of education and job placement.
- Invest in digital infrastructure and connectivity for underserved communities. Ensuring the availability of digital infrastructure for every student can bridge inequality and gaps in the educational system when linking access with education offerings and skill development programs.

Response from Dr. Kumar
Skilling is the need of the hour. We can't have enough because the demand for skilled labor is going to explode. However, it might be difficult and not feasible for everyone to be on the same platform. Benchmarking success will help to identify successful programs that can be supported for scaling with state and local governments. The NITI Aayog is open to designing those required metrics together with industry.

In order to provide underserved communities with digital infrastructure (e.g., digital devices and digital education), CSR funds from the industry could be leveraged instead of the government singlehandedly trying to achieve this. On this subject, Dr. Kumar raised the following questions that were addressed in the follow-up meeting in May 2022:

- What can be the metrics for benchmarking the success of a program?
- Where is the weak point of the national education policy?
- How can CSR funds be effectively used for digital education?

QUESTIONS FOR THE INDUSTRY – ADDRESSED AT THE FOLLOW-UP MEETING

1st Question: What can be the metrics for benchmarking the success of a program?

From the president of an Indian information technology company:

- Experiences from Mahindra University in Hyderabad suggest metrics for sustainable development. The model can follow the 17 SDGs where the major metrics could be in segments: facility & operations, teaching and curriculum, organizational management, community, research, assessment, and communication.

2nd Question: Where is the weak point of national education policy?

From the president of an Indian information technology company:

- There need to be multiple entry-exit points. The National Skill Development Policy is mainly suitable for early skill development and not for larger programs. Someone leaving after the first year of college does not make economic and pedagogic sense right now. Flexibility is missing.

- Enable change of mindset for digital education. Currently, digital education investments are made mainly in the classroom and equipment. Train teachers to deliver programs digitally and unlock boosts through digital enablement.
- From the CEO of the Indian branch of a European energy company:

From an outside perspective, India's educational system is doing very well in bringing up people who have broad knowledge. For my company, there are three major challenges:

- Have specific cluster knowledge. The system brings up people with broad knowledge instead of subject matter experts. The system needs to be more specific on clusters and tap into the whole potential of India.
- Have flexible and responsible talent. People are too focused on specific tasks. My company requires more flexible and responsible people in India to take these activities on-site rather than from our home country. Topics like hydrogen and storage need to be addressed, requiring flexible people to take on responsibility and execute these projects.
- Close education access gaps. Many people are not getting full access; my company's scholarship program tries to identify people who are not covered and bring them into the system. The CSR budget (2% of profits) can be used for workforce development, especially for underserved audiences.

From the CEO of an Indian hospital chain:

- No vertical integration of programs for credit transfer. Four ministries are currently involved in healthcare education and there is a lack of options to transfer credits between certificate programs across ministries. This causes a lack of aspiration among youth to become health workers.

- Keep up with the skills we need. Reskilling the healthcare workforce is required and an additional 1.5 million doctors are needed. State-level institutions need to align with approvals to train more nurses.
- Establish Blended Finance Frameworks to attract more investments in healthcare. Unlocking more capital for last-mile connectivity is crucial to enabling better healthcare services. Our partnership with the telecommunications industry is a success, but scale is needed. Investors need to understand the risk and long-term returns alongside securities. Blended finance frameworks such as social bonds and impact bonds need to be further developed through policy reforms, creating a streamlined process which will keep investors satisfied.

From the managing director of the South Asian branch of an American software company:

- Close access gap for villagers. Under the Bharat Net Program, more than 40% of the villages have yet to be connected to the internet, which creates a disadvantageous situation for rural students.
- Provide compulsory employability & entrepreneurship classes. The undergraduate program should teach employability skills and entrepreneurship respectively, apart from core subjects, non-core subjects, and elective subjects.
- Employ retired professors as research guides. Regardless of their age, retired professors should be used as research faculty to guide research scholars towards their Ph.D. This will eliminate the scarcity of research guides.

From an executive in the South Asian branch of an American software company:

- Learning platforms need to be uniform. There are many learning platforms with a good curriculum. Somebody needs to unify all content that can be delivered, and a new collaboration needs to be set up with every university. Learners are confused about where to get the right content.
- Lack of funds for pilot cases. CSR is not scalable and the government should enable large-scale investment alongside private investment. A PPP framework is needed to make this happen.

From an executive in an American technology company:

- Ensure student counseling. Proper counseling and sensitization is required to ensure that students from various backgrounds do not end up giving preference to diploma courses in the quest to realize earnings sooner.
- Minimize English language gaps. Policy focusing on regional languages for teaching academic courses in government schools might lead to the widening of existing gaps in English language skills.
- Overcome weak links. There is a lack of standards and technology infrastructure, as well as corporate/CSR and civil society initiatives.

3rd Question: How can CSR funds be effectively used for digital education?

From an executive in an American technology company:

- Scalability of programs comes with government dependency. While industry associations have also come forward to develop digital education programs per the government's skilling priorities, scaling up of these programs has remained a challenge. There is a growing dependence on federal or state-level support for mass adoption of such scalable programs at the university or state college level.

- Government as a key driver. Ideally, the government should shortlist/identify such CSR initiatives in skilling/education and provide the necessary impetus from the policy or adoption standpoint to widen its impact on the ground to bridge the skill gaps.
- From the managing director of the Indian branch of an American printing corporation:
- Bring in cutting-edge technology through CSR. We are eager to explore projects that will evaluate how CSR programs can be enabled for digital educational programs. We can also look at the possibilities of using our AR-based offering in enabling the entire education ecosystem.
- From an executive in the Southeast Asian branch of an American software corporation:
- Create initiatives to close 90 million of the skill gaps in manufacturing. Mechanical engineering discipline needs contributions for skilling next-gen designers and engineers, and CSR can provide this.
- Improve CSR feasibility in an educational program. My company is already investing in education with all software free of charge for educational purposes. We are happy to work on specific projects alongside the government, and we hope to collaborate with them for education on design, manufacturing, and information technology for ages up to 28.
- From the Head - Skills & Education of an American software company:
- Creativity is a foundational pillar for education that CSR can facilitate. My company already contributes by investing

heavily in Atel's innovation mission and other initiatives. Mentoring students one-on-one and earning credits that have an impact beyond the CSR initiative is important.

- Integrate of scores/credits as a success factor. Free-of-cost credits handed out by my company should be acknowledged by the educational system to have a real impact on a student's career.

Final Presentation #3: Last-mile Connectivity

This presentation was co-chaired by the president of an Indian telecommunications company and an Indian state government official, with contributions from over 20 executives from various industries. Here are the results of their discussion of last-mile connectivity:

Establishing Last-mile Connectivity

Outcome: Availability for all

Policy Intervention Required:
- Broadband for all programs should be carried out in a mission mode.
- Availability of sufficient spectrum resources.
- Benefits/Justification:
- Inclusive growth.
- Contribution to the economy from unconnected areas.
- Gender equality and empowerment of women.
- Rural entrepreneurship.
- Faster rollout of wireless networks and quicker benefits.
- India has one of the highest population densities, and therefore sufficient spectrum is critically required to create a quality network and sufficient capacity to support all use cases.

Outcome: Affordable connectivity

Policy Intervention Required:

- Affordable smartphone/broadband devices
- Reduction in taxes and levies
- Benefits/Justification:
- The cost of devices is a big entry barrier. Government should help provide smartphones/broadband devices for all.
- Broadband penetration leads to overall economic development of community. Therefore, government should reduce levies and taxes to make services affordable for all. The present levies are around 30% of the industry's revenue.

Outcome: Alignment of stakeholders for rolling out the network

Policy Intervention Required:

- Statutory provision for Right of Way to lay optical fiber and to build mobile infrastructure.
- Availability of power at affordable rates
- Benefits/Justification:
- RoW permission and charges are big barriers in network rollout. Timely and cost-effective RoW permissions lead to rollout of viable networks.
- Availability of power at reasonable rates is critical for the overall affordability of last-mile connectivity and quality/ uptime. Therefore, electricity distribution companies must provide power at affordable rates.

Outcome: Government's support in development of use cases

Policy Intervention Required:

- Government should support the rollout of various use cases, most importantly in the health, education, and agriculture sectors.
- Benefits/Justification:
- Many use cases, especially in rural areas, need viability gap funding in the initial stage before they become commercially viable.
- The support for such use cases provides the benefit to society and also makes the rollout of connectivity viable and affordable.
- Support for last mile in the health and education sectors is critical, as it leads to community development and security.
- Support for last mile in the agriculture sector helps to increase the contribution of rural areas to the overall economy.

Response from Dr. Kumar

Digital connectivity is very important. The government has announced that the private sector takes on execution through new tenders to accelerate connectivity, and the Prime Minister has been very committed to this. The fiber needs to reach all the Grand Pajans in the country, and households will then need to be connected. This is where private entrepreneurship will be critical to offering services.

At the end of 2023, all Grand Panjans (2,5 Lakh) will be connected to the fiber grid. Given the population density, it is unclear whether any amount of spectrum will be enough and whether 5G can be run on the available spectrum. Responsible ministries need to take up the issue. Optical fiber will be the answer to providing bandwidth, and new technology needs to be developed to bring down the cost of fiber. For this, the private sector should work with local government bodies to create synergy effects with the electricity grid infrastructure development. A parallel execution will eventually bring down costs and development time. This requires an extended discussion about what are the optimal solutions given the population's density and time urgency. Dr. Kumar raised the following questions that were addressed at the follow-up meeting in May, 2022:

- Provide cases on how utilization of connectivity in the villages has commercial value.
- Provide solutions for how to address the spectrum issue to ensure high broadband bandwidth.

Questions for the Industry – Addressed at the Follow-up Meeting

1ˢᵗ Question: Provide cases on how utilization of connectivity in the villages has commercial value.

From the CEO of the Indian branch of an American technology company:

- Over 200,000 villages have already been brought on to the optical fiber network and user numbers are growing quickly. The central government is looking at providing broadband access in 600K villages by 2025 under the Digital India program launched in 2015. The program seeks to improve citizens' access to government services through enhanced telecom infrastructure. India has 646 million active internet users aged 2 years and above as of December 2021. Rural India has 352 million internet users, almost 20% higher than urban areas. According to the study, the number of

Solomon Darwin with Yashraj Bhardwaj

active Internet users aged 12 years and above is 592 million. Compared with 2019, the active internet user base for 12 years and above has shown an impressive growth of ~37%. Rural users' growth at 45% continues to outshine urban users' growth at 28% over 2019. Female users' growth in the last two years is a whopping 61% as compared to male users who grew at 24%.

- My company's development project bridges gaps. We are engaging in a technology initiative to bring middle-mile connectivity to rural India through a simple, affordable solution leveraging electric cables. Connectivity enables access to information and a host of services, from ecommerce platforms for entrepreneurs to financing, digital payments, telemedicine, online education, entertainment, and more, all of which spur economic activity and progress for the rural community. According to a study by the World Bank, every 10 percentage-point increase in broadband penetration provides a boost of 1.38 additional percentage points to GDP growth, higher than any other telecommunication service.

From the co-founder and Chief Business Officer of an Indian financial services company:

- Digitalization can help rural regions overcome some of their traditional challenges. Low density and shrinking local markets are two of the main bottlenecks for long-term sustainability in many rural economies. Digitalization can offer new growth possibilities and opportunities for better and more diversified jobs in rural regions. Some effects of the digital age that can provide a boost for rural regions are reduction of trade times and costs, the exchange of new types of products and services, access to global markets, and disruptive ways to work and join the labor market.

- The digital age can modify how firms provide non-tradable services. Traditionally, the exchange of non-tradable services (e.g., law, health, or hairdressers) occurs through face-to-face contact (getting a vaccine or a haircut). However, some researchers have claimed that emerging technologies like virtual or augmented reality can make face-to-face contactless relevant for the exchange of non-tradable services.
- New technologies can enhance the entrepreneurial business environment in rural economies. Technological progress has the potential to spur innovation in rural communities. Greater interaction among firms and people facilitates innovation processes. Online platforms and blockchain technologies directly link businesses to workers and customers, enabling the emergence of new forms of employment/entrepreneurship.
- Policies need to support commercialization. Ensure high-quality broadband in all rural regions. Strengthen infrastructure (telecommunications infrastructure and roads). Upskill the labor force. Develop forward-looking policies and regulations with greater involvement of rural communities.

2ⁿᵈ Question: Provide solutions for how to address the spectrum issue to ensure high broadband bandwidth.

From the president of an Indian telecommunications company:

- Rural connectivity and last-mile connectivity come with unique end-user characteristics. The mobile device is the first device to get online as 98% 4G penetration lets people use mobile. Thus, people don't understand the value of fiber. However, TV is the first demand to come onboard on fiber and can be the start for other use cases.

- Revenue is a challenge. Revenue potential in villages is very low, and this needs to be considered. Public tenders for fiber implementation don't create much interest for the industry since there are no revenue streams. Other incentives may improve traction.

- Spectrum needs to become more flexible for various cases. The volume of GB is increasing and increases demand for bandwidth. There are various compartments in the spectrum, but the broadband spectrum is limited. India should adopt a dynamic strategy where the spectrum can be used flexibly. The U.S. is following such an approach to increase the utilization of the spectrum. Industry can buy spectrum and use it in various cases, just as diesel can be used for various vehicles.

DR. KUMAR'S FINAL SUMMARY AND FEEDBACK

Dr. Kumar expressed gratitude for this feedback session and encouraged the attendees to contribute to policy making even more outside the NITI Aayog. The Prime Minister had asked Dr. Kumar for his input regarding policymaking going forward, and this initiative will help provide continuous input to advance India. For this feedback session, Dr. Kumar summarized the following points.

- **Skill Gap:** A huge skill gap exists, and demand cannot be estimated for different skills. Work should be done in each state to determine the true skill demand. Skill mapping to forecast demand and match it with supply should be done. Female digital literacy is another major issue that prevents increasing female labor participation, and reasons for this situation need to be found. India aspires to become a global supplier of skills, and every recommendation from the conference is well taken.

- **Compliance:** It is good to hear from the participants that the compliance problem has improved. As always, there are miles to go. However, compliance issues, such as lack of synchronization between central and state governments, insufficient online systems, and conflict between old and new rules, need to be solved at the state level. Therefore, Dr. Kumar asked the forum to think of state-specific innovation and investment forums to address challenges more effectively.

- **Talent Flexibility & National Education Policy:** All ministries are engaged in the implementation and rollout of the national education policy, which is an ambitious and complicated one. Grades and credits are in the process of being transferred, and each state has a unique case. Implementation for each state is urgent and necessary. Dr. Kumar concluded that education needs to be increased online as well as off. MOOCS and digital education need to scale. However, he doubts that standardization can be done uniformly across India. Every part of the country needs different styles and requirements, and several large platforms would be more feasible than one.

- **Connectivity:** Constitutional provisions may make it difficult to create policy. Why not work with the state governments instead of a centralized approach? The flexibility of the spectrum is a very good suggestion. It remains an open question how to operationalize this technical task. Dr.

Kumar invited more details on technical and commercial feasibility.

- **Pollution Control Board:** The central pollution control board needs to be simplified and rationalized. There should be an independent unit that constantly engages with business leaders and ministry with persistence and perseverance. Only then may modernization and improvements happen. It is all about framing this in a policy-friendly manner and then pushing it to make it happen.

- **Blended Finance for Health:** This is an important objective. Such innovation should come from the private sector in collaboration with the financial operators and agents. The government should not involve itself at first, only entering the picture later with execution and support to increase attractiveness.

- **Green Manufacturing:** There is a global consensus that going green is a public good. Countries like India can be assisted to make the transition happen because India needs to develop while transforming. We might want to bring in some global resources. There is a $10 billion fund from the Gates Foundation. The industry should also look for outside money, not solely from the government of India.

- **Going Forward:**
    o   Form small groups of people who can engage with different agencies to push this agenda forward.
    o   Create a public narrative to influence policymakers.
    o   Engage with state governments rather than just the central one because of their sheer size (as compared to single EU countries).
    o   Think of a few state-level subsidiaries to hold forums on specific challenges that can be addressed.

AUTHOR'S REMARKS: LEVERAGING THE BIFI ECOSYSTEM TO POWER INDIA'S GROWTH

Werner Fischer (Consultant, Advisor & Author Catalyze Group & UC Berkeley) offered the following remarks:

The Berkeley Innovation Forum India (BIFI) provides a unique opportunity to power India's growth. Over the last two days, prestigious leaders have discussed ideas and strategies on how to take the three initiatives forward with compassion, great will to commit resources, and a strong belief in transforming India into a center of innovation. The combined knowledge, associated assets, and commitment to drive real change have resulted in strategies and action plans that now wait for their real-life application.

Ecosystems have been proven to change the world. It was the collaboration between the highly innovative German start-up BioNTech and one of the largest U.S. pharma groups, Pfizer, that enabled the speedy commercialization of one of the first highly effective COVID vaccines. Looking at this year's Berkeley Innovation Forum India creates a great urge to kickstart similar, powerful ecosystems to change India in manufacturing, education, and digital connectivity. The BIFI provides not only some of the best multinationals, start-ups, and SMEs in the world of industry but also best-in-class academics and bureaucrats.

Moving forward, I encourage the NITI Aayog and UC Berkeley to shepherd the process of bringing partners together and creating impact in each initiative. UC Berkeley's agnostic, nonprofit-driven position allows building trust and alignment among participants while supporting world-class research capabilities and market linkages. The NITI Aayog's unique position allows innovation to align with policymaking and find its way quickly to the market and end users. It is this triple-helix structure powered by open innovation that provides a unique and powerful pathway to India's bright future.

My recommendations for driving this initiative forward include:

- Formulate specific objectives and key results for each initiative.
- Orchestrate and finalize partner consortia.
- Finalize action plans and budgets ready for execution.
- Define business models and how co-developed IP should be distributed and commercialized among partners.
- Establish an open innovation governance structure to ensure ongoing feedback loops with stakeholders.
- Innovate through agile sprints and quickly commercialize to create measurable impact.

AUTHOR'S REMARKS: IMPORTANCE OF GOVERNMENT AS THE FIRST MOVER AND STAGE SETTER FOR THE OVERALL VISION

The next speaker was Yashraj Bhardwaj (Advisor & Garwood Fellow, Haas School of Business, UC Berkeley; Co-Founder and Director, Petonic Infotech):

Change is a major part of our lives, whether it is change in industries, technologies or sectors such as transportation, education, health care, or social policies. But we still know little about when and how change occurs. Policy refers to a broad statement that reflects future goals and aspirations and provides guidelines for carrying out those goals. Scientists argue that policy formulation is a process and not a one-time affair. Public policies also do not evolve with the activities of top-level executives alone; instead, they involve the active participation of non-political groups, private players, civil society organizations, and so on. Thus, the process of policy formulation involves negotiation, bargaining, and accommodation of many different interests, which eventually becomes a policy with the process of legitimizing.

The process of policy formulation and development is not simple, but a complex and continuously changing one that is conditioned by a multitude of factors. A good policy formulation process is one "which is committed to producing a high-quality decision – not any particular decision." Such a decision should be made with a high degree of legitimacy, power, and accuracy. Hence, to produce such a high-quality decision, the policy formulation process should possess certain characteristic features. I firmly believe that India as a country has succeeded thanks to the government being the first mover and stage setter of the overall vision for successful formations, implementations of policies through guidance, and continuous policy formulation in the changing landscape.

The greatest danger in times of turbulence is not the turbulence – it is to act with yesterday's logic. The diversification and increase in complexity of technologies, trends, and both their manifestation at the societal level and direct impact on individuals, families, and communities make policymaking fraught with concerns about how to achieve stated goals in a fair and balanced way that holds up to scrutiny. The government as a policymaker needs to decode both the impact and the trajectory of these technologies and trends on their core constituents. Merely comprehending the bits and bytes, nuts and bolts is simply not enough. Furthermore, merely understanding these aspects is only part of the tasks before policymakers. They need to also grapple with the topics that are side effects but serious in their import.

There needs to be a mindset that is open to novelty and disruptive approaches to policy making, which looks to maximize the benefit for the whole rather than the few. Government has a crucial role to play throughout the policy-making lifecycle to ensure that implementation follows suit, not only regarding the details but also in line with the overarching societal goals to enhance India's performance when it comes to sustainability, security, and prosperity.

The Rebuilding India Initiative is all about building an ecosystem to create trust that enables and facilitates scaling and reinvigoration of the Indian economy. The first stakeholder, the initiator, contributor, and catalyst of this goal, would be the government. The government has the capacity and competency to understand the incentives, interests, and concerns that different stakeholders have, which is the first step in cracking this puzzle of rebuilding India.

RECOMMENDED ACTION PLANS BY INDIVIDUAL COMPANIES

What follows are the individual action plans by the companies and organizations that served as the baseline for discussion to develop the final presentation for each of the three initiatives discussed (manufacturing, education, and last-mile connectivity).

EDUCATION RECOMMENDATIONS FROM THE CTO OF AN AMERICAN SOFTWARE COMPANY

Provide four critical success factors to take the initiative forward

- Infrastructure – power, internet, work stations, sanitation, meeting spaces.
- National Credential System – standardized skills, testing, badging.
- National Employer Job Pool and Mentoring Network – placement into jobs with assistance from mentors and the appropriate jobs to fill – also a system to track key process areas.
- Financial support from the government and business.

What do you need from the government?

- Funding.
- Support for a national credential system.
- Infrastructure support.
- Tax and business incentives for corporations to participate.

What do you need from your corporate ecosystem players?

- Support for funding, resources, and pro bono work.
- Job curriculum development on an open platform.
- A job board and posting available openings.

What do you need from UC Berkeley?

- Benchmarking of companies participating. How are the companies more successful as a result of participation?

- Identification and tracking key process areas – what measures define success, and are we successful?

What do you recommend as the next steps?
Take action by securing funding for additional labs in an area such as Meghalaya; they have already shown success at two labs connected with our initiative.

EDUCATION RECOMMENDATIONS FROM AN EXECUTIVE IN THE SOUTHEAST ASIAN BRANCH OF AN AMERICAN SOFTWARE COMPANY

Provide four critical success factors to take the initiative forward

- Digitization of curriculum.
- Industry needs and requirements for job readiness.
- Building a scalable ecosystem to drive skilling in the broader ecosystem.
- Certification and assessment for specific job roles.

What do you need from the government?

- AICTE curriculum framework to be aligned to project-based learning outcomes.
- Introducing credit in programs.
- One body responsible for implementation to achieve the above SCFs.

What do you need from your corporate ecosystem players?

- Ask customers to pair with academia to solve real-time industry problems.
- All stakeholders should work together to build a vision document on skilling.

What do you need from UC Berkeley?

- Identify priority sector skills to develop talent (objectives and goals).
- Replicate global best practices in India.

- Endorse action plan and work with the NITI Aayog to get the required government approvals, including budgets.

What do you recommend as the next steps?

- Form a consortium with key stakeholders to build the strategic and implementation plan for skilling youth.

EDUCATION RECOMMENDATIONS FROM AN EXECUTIVE AT AN AMERICAN SOFTWARE COMPANY

Provide four critical success factors to take the initiative forward

- Move fast and at scale from policy and recommendation to action.
- Readiness and capacity to scale - assess the level of education, region, and language.
- Consolidation of jurisdiction from different initiatives across several government ministries and departments.
- Flexibility and agility in systems and processes such as academic credentialing and accreditation.

What do you need from the government?

- Speedier execution from policy to implementation.
- Agility and flexibility in allowing innovation in the educational ecosystem and tech.
- Inclusion of in-demand courses at the curriculum design level.
- Permission for the micro-accreditation system to recognize non-formal education.
- Closure of the critical digital skill gap (my company has the opportunity to create 1-3 million jobs and $66 billion in revenue by 2026, directly and indirectly, if skilled talent is available).

What do you need from your corporate ecosystem players?

- Participate and offer experiential- and application-based learning for potential job seekers, students, and educators/faculty.
- Help governments scale up beyond selected colleges.
- Provide more aid and courses at school level.
- Adopt a flexible approach in joining hands with fellow industry players to benefit from network effects – open business model and open innovation.
- Afford greater flexibility to startups to create solutions and unlock more innovation.

What do you need from UC Berkeley?

- Create a compendium of best practices across the Triple Helix System.
- Act on recommendations proposed in this forum to become actionable.

MANUFACTURING RECOMMENDATIONS FROM THE CEO OF AN INDIAN MANAGEMENT CONSULTING FIRM

General Challenges

- Lack of developed manufacturing ecosystem in India, inefficient resource allocation mechanism, presence mostly in assembling at full scale.
  - o There are a limited number of Indian companies involved in manufacturing of mobile phones and sub-assemblies; also low production operations by foreign firms established in India, with more focus on assembly operations.
  - o Assembly activities are on the rise for smartphones but still at a low scale, much lower in the case of computer hardware.
  - o While global firms such as Xiaomi, Samsung, Apple, and Vivo have made initial investments in India, they fail to penetrate much due to a lack of developed manufacturing base in India and lack of a sufficient scale (unlike China or Vietnam).
  - o Overall, there is a weak domestic ecosystem and value chains in areas such as industrial and consumer electronics, which lack policy impetus.
- Infrastructure and logistic related issues even in terms of costs
  - o There is a lack of mega manufacturing clusters and accompanying infrastructure.
  - o There is an erratic power supply and polluted water sources.

- o There need to be significant transportation facilities for sending finished products to ports, as many primary mobile manufacturing hubs (i.e., Uttarakhand, Delhi, Haryana, Uttar Pradesh, and Telangana) are inland. This adds to costs.
- Limited designing activities & presence of fabs in India – a must for the growth of Indian electronics
  - o India lacks competence in chip design; there are very few semiconductor fab units in the country, despite NPE's focus on chip design.
  - o The Semi-Conductor Laboratory (SCL) established at Chandigarh only has a 28-nanometer fab, which needs to be upgraded to 65-nanometer and 228-nanometer.
  - o India isn't strong at designing electronic items in GVCs, but these are required to support manufacturing systems.
- Insufficient labor skills and persistent demand-supply gap
  - o The need for specialized skills has increased owing to greater technological complexities (IoT, AI); despite the rise in demand for skilled workers and design engineers, the supply of such workers is still not sufficient.
  - o The country is compelled to rely on other nations, such as China, for technicians who specialize in the setup of sophisticated machinery and technical assistance.
  - o Higher expenses on reskilling workers raise manufacturing costs.
  - o Labor laws are not industry-friendly.
  - o There is a lack of proper design institutes which can generate skills for this industry

Suggestions on R&D clusters

- More investment on data and research. The non-availability of databases for Indian electronics production (value and volume terms) at a disaggregated level is a major limitation for undertaking credible analysis. Empirically, there is also a lack of detailed analysis of state governments' policies and a paucity of studies on value chain analysis for key electronic items for India, such as smartphones, TVs, PCs, and laptops. MeitY and MoPSI, working together with other policy think tanks in the country, should make data collection and data availability to researchers a priority, to fill in the existing gaps.

- The decision to reduce dependency on China needs to be strategic and meticulously planned. Some economic interdependencies between India and China are not only inevitable but desirable in a globalized world. But if geopolitical considerations call for reducing these dependencies, such decisions need to be informed by deep analysis of the global supply chain ecosystem in electronics. One strategy will be to develop lead firms in domestic value chains to capture a higher share of the pie in GVCs over time. However, to develop India's electronics manufacturing ecosystem in the interim, GVCs based in China should be encouraged to expand to India. They have the required expertise, technical knowledge, and experience to build manufacturing capacities and scale within a short period of time. Experience suggests that these lead firms move with their ecosystem. Preventing the GVC ecosystems to shift will not only stifle large scale production, but also adversely impact domestic value addition, as lead firms will turn to imports for components.

- Industrial policy can best succeed in a pro-trade and pro-market environment. In the short run, India should try to reap the maximum benefits from existing GVCs and from its current FTAs, and also explore new trade partners and scale up assembly activities in smartphones. All efforts need to be directed to build competitiveness domestically and to drive exports. Linking to GVCs, as well as inviting more FDI inflows, requires a liberalized yet stable environment with a focus on reducing the cost of doing business. Interventions include:

o Moving away from traditional subsidies to production or exports-based incentives, along with a single window clearance.

o Enforcement mechanisms and IP systems should be strengthened to plug gray market operations in the case of high-end mobile phones.

o There should be time-bound efforts for R&D with high-funding options for fabs.

o An enhanced partnership between academia, government and the private sector can help to pool knowledge, strategies and finance.

EDUCATION RECOMMENDATIONS FROM AN EXECUTIVE AT AN AMERICAN SOFTWARE COMPANY

Provide some critical success factors to take the initiative forward

- Create an open ecosystem where knowledge can be stored.
- Remove bottlenecks for startups.
- Ease accessibility of funds for POCs.

What do you need from the government?

The government is doing a great job, but it is a long road and we need to plan how small companies can flourish in the Make in India Initiative. We should plan 50,000 companies with 10 Cr revenue.

What do you need from your corporate ecosystem players?

The corporate ecosystem needs to create trust and take ownership to mentor and help smaller players to develop products for markets.

What do you need from UC Berkeley?

Identify the social problems existing in India and then connect them to the VC ecosystem to help find solutions for them.

MANUFACTURING RECOMMENDATIONS FROM A DATA SCIENTIST AT AN AMERICAN TECHNOLOGY COMPANY

Provide some critical success factors to take the initiative forward

- Invest in the infrastructure required by the electronics automotive manufacturing industry (port, roads, electricity, water).
- Encourage private industry to invest in manufacturing of parts, subassemblies, and life-cycle support of products.
- Simplify the approval licensing process for international players who can invest and establish manufacturing facilities in India.

What do you need from the government?
It must facilitate and simplify the process and could offer incentives (e.g., subsidize land and power).

What do you need from your corporate ecosystem players?
Electronics and automotive industry organizations must offer paid training and internships to fresh graduates from educational institutions to help develop skills.

What do you need from UC Berkeley?
UC Berkeley could open an India School of Engineering offering similar courses as in Berkeley at one or more institutes in India. This would provide students with specialized classes to develop skills in electronics and automotive manufacturing.

Solomon Darwin with Yashraj Bhardwaj

EDUCATION RECOMMENDATIONS FROM THE CEO OF AN AMERICAN STARTUP

Provide some critical success factors to take the initiative forward

- Move away from siloed processes to make sure that resources, policies, and strategies are made available to all stakeholders.
- This includes standardizing for scale and mass adoption of policies such as micro credentials that are recognized by all companies and universities.
- Continued dialogue after the forum is over, with sustained relationships and cross-collaboration to keep communication channels open between all stakeholders.

What do you need from the government?
Vernacular asset mapping in India that is made available to the private sector for open innovation so that we can see synergies between the social, cultural, and creative assets of different villages/locations. This will help us understand how to scale solutions for connectivity, education, and manufacturing. It will also show the contrasting needs of localized communities and expose barriers that cause solutions to fail.

What do you need from your corporate ecosystem players?

- More dialogue with startups that share a mutual mission but have distinguished offerings.
- To provide more efficient funding channels for startup projects and to accelerate impact, rather than Fortune 500 companies duplicating efforts and offerings by always building in-house solutions that compete instead of collaborating.

What do you need from UC Berkeley?

- Recognize micro credentials.
- More consultation with industry to identify the changing skills needed for the future of work.
- Connecting students with industry for more cross-collaboration.

MANUFACTURING RECOMMENDATIONS FROM THE GENERAL MANAGER OF THE INDIAN BRANCH OF A EUROPEAN SECURITY EQUIPMENT COMPANY

Provide four critical success factors to take the initiative forward

- We will require much larger participation from sections of society to make this initiative holistic.
- When we have to push manufacturing in India, we need to get the MSME involved.
- The different arms of the government (center, state, different departments such as industry and taxation) need to have a single policy for manufacturing. Today, they are not in sync.
- We as a country need to work on factors like labor rules, electricity availability, and logistical costs.

What do you need from the government?

- Labor reforms consistent across states.
- Logistics cost and time reduction.
- Synchronization in different ministries while developing policy.

What do you need from your corporate ecosystem players?

- Create an atmosphere of cooperation.
- Break some of the cartels, like cement and steel, which engage in price-fixing.
- Collaborate with companies that produce essential materials.

What do you need from UC Berkeley?

- Share how open-source innovation happened in Silicon Valley.
- Enable the creation of a similar atmosphere in India.
- Aid the development of industry-academia engagement in India.

What do you recommend as the next steps?

Have follow-up meetings to gain input and create an ecosystem mechanism of all the decisions that will be made.

Solomon Darwin with Yashraj Bhardwaj

MANUFACTURING RECOMMENDATIONS FROM A VICE PRESIDENT AT A EUROPEAN ENERGY COMPANY

Provide four critical success factors to take the initiative forward

- Visible action and task forcing of mutually-agreed initiatives by industry, government, and academia.
- Smart KPIs can be measured, demonstrated, and reviewed to create deeper engagements as they progress.
- Align global trends and ambitions within the country; build capability and augmentation to develop a unified action.
- Manufacturing hub should focus on green energy (Power to X) initiative, including green hydrogen economy as the largest Forex driver.

What do you need from the government?

- Build a National Hydrogen Policy. A consumption mandate will facilitate quicker and more sustainable capacity building by industry players.
- Create mandatory requirements for decarbonized industry, leading to the development of non-fossil/non-gas options.

What do you need from your corporate ecosystem players?

- The focus on a decarbonized industry needs an entire ecosystem of alternate fuel development and heat recycling solutions and providers.
- SMART factory – IOT connected manufacturing ecosystem – creating edge connectivity for cloud analytics – focus on sensors/device manufacturing.

- Create standardized interfaces for seamless controls and access to field devices. Reinforce open protocols.

What do you need from UC Berkeley?

- Work with startups beyond the U.S., focusing on European and Indian institutions as well.
- Broaden the horizon beyond digital corporations; the industry needs more dimensions to realize the three stated objectives (workmen, technicians, engineers).

What do you recommend as the next steps?

- Engagement depth should increase with task force creation beyond CXO engagements.

Solomon Darwin with Yashraj Bhardwaj

LAST-MILE CONNECTIVITY RECOMMENDATIONS FROM AN INDIAN STATE GOVERNMENT REPRESENTATIVE

Provide four critical success factors to take the initiative forward

- Clarify the purpose and goals to all stakeholders.
- Work in a mission mode with a collaborative approach.
- Bring enabling policy framework to realize the goals and mission.
- Build social capital at the last mile to ensure social inclusion and unlock the full potential of the bottom of the pyramid.

What do you need from the government?

- Corporations need to understand the local problems and local solutions. The idea is not to sell products but to develop solutions.
- Understand the concept of diversity within diversity.

What do you need from your corporate ecosystem players?

- Alignment and goals to see that corporations and the government work together to achieve a purpose.
- Greater ease of doing business.

What do you need from UC Berkeley?

- Nurture Triple Helix Model.
- Scale up Smart Village Movement project.

What do you recommend as the next steps?
Launch the mission to connect and empower last-mile populations.

MANUFACTURING RECOMMENDATIONS FROM THE GENERAL MANAGER OF THE SOUTH INDIAN BRANCH OF AN AMERICAN TECHNOLOGY COMPANY

Provide four critical success factors to take the initiative forward

- Make provisions for local manufacturers in the public procurement process throughout the tenure of the PLI scheme.
- Lower compliance burdens such as CRO approvals and e-waste of customs to increase the ease of doing business.
- Build the component ecosystem manufacturing in India.
- Create robust and sustainable skill development programs in partnership with the industry.

What do you need from the government?

- Encourage state governments to participate in procurement.
- Extend PLI regime from 4 to 6 years of increase in annual incentive fee.

What do you need from your corporate ecosystem players?

- Build a consortium to achieve common goals.
- Make investments to develop indigenous technology locally.
- Keep nation building as a key corporate priority to encourage the next level of leadership.
- Co-create new products and solutions, making them affordable and increasing speed in the market.

What do you need from UC Berkeley?

- Bring this agenda on a continuous basis of recommendation for all actions that need to be taken in a timely manner.
- Help seek investments and budgets to modernize India.

What do you recommend as the next steps?

Continue to build on these actions and review measurable outcomes. Ensure that this consortium meets on a more frequent and regularly-scheduled basis to achieve common goals.

EDUCATION RECOMMENDATIONS FROM A SENIOR VICE PRESIDENT AT AN INDIAN HEALTHCARE GROUP

Provide four critical success factors to take the initiative forward

- Build on current success stories and initiatives.
- Identify the gaps/breaks in scaling up.
- Build key denominators for digital, skills, and finance that are necessary for any outcome.
- Get champions to lead with concrete projects.

What do you need from the government?

- Enable projects to be scaled up across states and nationwide.
- Partner in accelerating outcomes.
- Position India as a successful provider of products and services.

What do you need from your corporate ecosystem players?

- Share your stories and successes to create a playbook.
- Converge with partners to achieve capacity building and best outcomes.
- Work closely with the government for a policy ecosystem that helps achieve outcomes.

What do you need from UC Berkeley?

- Aid in identifying successes and constraints for playbooks.
- Work with corporations and create case studies for global partnering.

What do you recommend as the next steps?
Create a timeline for action.

EDUCATION RECOMMENDATIONS FROM THE CEO OF THE INDIAN BRANCH OF AN AMERICAN BEVERAGE COMPANY

Provide four critical success factors to take the initiative forward

- The national policies must be backed with an open mind both by corporations and at public events to build trust and create joint forces for progress.
- Public infrastructure.
- Resolution of service provider issues.
- Last-mile digital connectivity.

What do you need from the government?

- Local government support.
- A mindset change.
- Fiscal incentives.

What do you need from your corporate ecosystem players?

- Jointly driving out each program to scale up impact (the idea to host educational programs on GitHub is great).
- Driving curriculum change at schools and universities in partnership with corporations.

What do you need from UC Berkeley?

- Supporting and driving curriculum change.
- Support in creating a study to set up a baseline.

What do you recommend as the next steps?
Plan for a study to set up a baseline for a segmented approach.

MANUFACTURING RECOMMENDATIONS FROM AN EXECUTIVE AT AN INDIAN CONGLOMERATE

Provide four critical success factors to take the initiative forward

- Make schools/teachers in government schools more skilled/updated/responsible/equipped
- Reduce government approvals and simplify the process for necessary ones.
- Improve infrastructure. Speed up GRATISHAKTI; improve access and support like "Design Knowledge" for MSME electronics manufacturers.
- Facilitate and catalyze academia-industry collaboration.

What are your asks from the government?
Work on the above success factors.

What are your asks from UC Berkeley?
Facilitate and push the government to achieve the objectives set above.

What do you recommend as the next steps?
Form small teams of representatives from government (ministries), corporations, and UC Berkeley suitably empowered to push and achieve objectives.

MANUFACTURING RECOMMENDATIONS FROM A VICE PRESIDENT AT THE SOUTH ASIAN BRANCH OF A EUROPEAN CONSUMER GOODS COMPANY

Provide four critical success factors to take the initiative forward

- Interdependency between the three objectives/workstream when fleshed out; this will give common goals to put combined actions.
- Involvement of missing industries to make this effort complete.
- The commercial business case is the only way to attract investments and encourages experimentation to scale up.
- Continued deployment of the helix model and ownership of the agenda between industry, academia, and government.

What do you need from the government?

- Make a plan for these three initiatives, set up a governance structure, and mount it with all participants to track progress.
- Unlock international technology partnerships.

What do you need from your corporate ecosystem players?

- Apart from supporting these initiatives in an individual company capacity, we should aim to collaborate and network to create capabilities together.

- Identify as a group of industries (due to inherent interdependencies of material) the top 10 materials that as a country we want to balk at and integrate. This will help us reduce Forex and international supply chain exposure.

What do you need from UC Berkeley?
Remain a guide/mentor to the initiative.

What do you recommend as the next steps?
Develop a detailed execution plan with critical milestones and resources required.

Notes on skill development
It is critical to evaluate and create ambition for how the talent of today can grow in value for tomorrow. It would be significant for both employment and entrepreneurship. Without this analysis and point of view, we could have demand-supply gaps.

Clear segmentation of the problem that we are trying to solve is critical. The broad education opportunities need to be understood for content creation (how many people will be students, uneducated youth, dropouts, etc.).

EDUCATION RECOMMENDATIONS FROM A VICE PRESIDENT AT THE SOUTH ASIAN BRANCH OF A EUROPEAN SOFTWARE COMPANY

Provide four critical success factors to take the initiative forward

- Identify and prioritize key industries of priority and high growth potential for India in the next 25 years (for example, agritech, renewable energy).
- Create industry-specific digital skilling ecosystem hubs in each of the four corners and the heart of India.
- Each ecosystem hub should include academia and government (supply side), and the digital technology industry with four key players (demand side).
- Have a 5-year mission with annual measures/metrics/targets based on a real-time data baseline combined with transparent reporting for continuous improvement and course correction.

What do you need from the government?

Create a single agency that will be responsible to drive/own the removal of all barriers called out by the ecosystem hubs within weeks.

What do you need from your corporate ecosystem players?

The demand side of education (employers) should plan and share their skills needs (immediate, short, medium, and long-term) with the digital technology industry and academia on a real-time and continuous basis.

What do you need from UC Berkeley?
Be an enabler for democratizing soft skill learning across the second- and third-tier universities, and even more importantly in the public education K-12 system.

What do you recommend as the next steps?

- Gather current data.
- Make a start now.
- Don't strategize too much; start small with an ecosystem that is more ready than others.

MANUFACTURING RECOMMENDATIONS FROM THE FORMER CEO OF A EUROPEAN INDUSTRIAL ENGINEERING CORPORATION

Provide four critical success factors to take the initiative forward

- Building greater trust between government and private sector through outreach. Don't overregulate; provide simple and stable policy frameworks
- Simplifying governance/increase ease of doing business: reduce compliance burden, labor laws, land acquisition.
- Increasing India's cost competitiveness: infrastructure development, energy costs.
- Creating targeted incentives for environmentally sustainable growth: green hydrogen, solar/wind renewables, e-mobility.

What do you need from the government?

- Build a mutually beneficial partnership with the industry based on trust (investments, jobs, exports).
- Develop a greater focus on infrastructure development (jobs, cost competitiveness).

What do you need from your corporate ecosystem players?
Create a framework for collaboration across the entire value chain for green hydrogen:

- Funding/scale/integration
- Manufacturing of green hydrogen (operations and technology providers)

- Storage
- Transportation
- User industries

What do you need from UC Berkeley?

- Identify a few specific high-impact projects for the NITI Aayog under each initiative.
- Facilitate the initiatives to enable traction.
- Promote greater collaboration with academia.

What do you recommend as the next steps?
Create a project plan and key milestones.

MANUFACTURING RECOMMENDATIONS FROM AN EXECUTIVE AT AN AMERICAN ELECTRONICS COMPANY

By and large, we find that the Indian landscape has transformed and is wonderfully supportive of proposals when presented with appropriate reasoning. There are some on-ground aberrations which need to be carefully isolated and corrected to build success stories and confidence in the investors.

- Aggressively capture and nurture anchor accounts.
  - o Tight windows of opportunity
  - o Contested by other countries
  - o Capture value without getting bogged down by concepts like product manufacturing vs. contract engineering
- Fast-track processing of anchor projects with aggressive elimination of bureaucratic red tape.
  - o My company had its first SPECS application acknowledged in three weeks! This speaks volumes for India's speed of execution.
  - o However, the second application had a minor debate on whether it was manufacturing or contract engineering. This is under favorable consideration and will definitely get cleared, but investment made before acknowledgment will not be eligible for incentives.
- Size of commitment does not matter to MNCs; once there is an agreement, aim at delivering the product easily and in a time-bound manner to inspire confidence.
  - o Unfortunately, the process of incentive release is often convoluted and the inspector who is clearing the incentive seems to see his role as that of a person who is saving the nation money by finding reasons why the incentive

should not be disbursed. It is easy for him to put an observation on record – and then most people will not make a decision in a hurry. It takes a lot of time to get this correct, and such delays have costs. However, the person who has caused the delay has no cost. The system should have a mechanism for holding such people accountable for the damage that they cause.

The government modified the SPECS policy in record time to address specific inputs we had given for enabling our sector. We resubmitted the application. As of now, we have our SPECS application acknowledged, which means that we can invest. If it is approved, all investments after the acknowledgment will be entitled to a government grant.

We have started our project on land which is leased for 5 years. We have also invested $50 million and bought another plot of land where we will build our engineering centers; we plan to move there in five years, extending the lease on the first plot of land only if there is a delay. However, there is an indication that we may be asked to amend our first lease to 10 years. Given that we have already bought the second plot of land, we hope that sanity will prevail and the unnecessary hassle and cost of extending the lease on the initial starting point will not become an issue.

MANUFACTURING RECOMMENDATIONS FROM THE CEO OF THE INDIAN BRANCH OF A EUROPEAN ENERGY COMPANY

Specific suggestions to support the development of a local manufacturing hub for renewable energy:
Domestic manufacturing is key to the success of renewable energy in India in meeting the government's ambitious plans of a 500 GW capacity target by 2030 and also making India an export hub for equipment. Specific suggestions in this regard are provided below for consideration:

- Further enhance ease of doing business: Provide single-window clearance for approvals within a specific timeframe of two or three months (or deemed approval if approval is delayed beyond this timeframe) to set up a manufacturing facility or associated supply systems. Also, set up an inter-ministerial body for ministries with overlapping mandates to work in tandem.
- Clear policy framework: With visibility for the next five to seven years in terms of regulations, policies and tax structures should enable manufacturers to take long-term capital investment decisions
- Tax concessions: Lower corporate income tax rate, lower GST on supplies and services, at least for the initial period until critical mass is established.
- Priority sector lending at lower interest rate: Priority sector lending for RE manufacturing provides access to low-cost capital.
- Duty exemptions: Import duty exemptions on equipment imports are required for setting up manufacturing lines and concessions on export duties.

- Accelerated depreciation: Accelerated depreciation benefits for approximately 10 years to recover investments more quickly.
- Create Special Economic Zones and accord benefits to support industry and other associated businesses around a cluster.
- Infrastructure facilities: Dedicated feeders for uninterrupted supply of power, water availability for process, facilitating land acquisition or providing land like a park at nominal charges and providing incentives like no registration charges, no non-agriculture (NA) land conversion requirements.
- PLI schemes: Increase Production Linked Incentives (PLI) schemes to incentivize more participation.
- R&D: Creation of R&D hubs with funding from government to encourage self-sufficiency in raw materials and create substitutes for imported materials. Public Sector Undertakings (PSUs) such as Bharat Heavy Electricals Limited (BHEL) and Bharat Electronics Limited (BEL) could be encouraged to lead solar manufacturing indigenisation efforts. Further, R&D should be encouraged in collaboration with international research centers, leading companies in the sector and start-ups with the aim of developing new recycling processes for end-of-life PV modules management through the recovery and reuse of materials in a fully circular perspective. For example, the use of highly automated procedures and sophisticated artificial intelligence algorithms will greatly improve the control of manufacturing processes, leading to significant scrap minimization.
- Create more demand for RE power: More stringent RPO implementation and local content requirement conditions in tenders. Also provide incentives like wheeling and

banking and encourage third-party sale for RE power. This increase would incentivize development of local manufacturing facilities.

Providing similar incentives for associated industries related to manufacturing of ingots, wafers, cells, back sheet, glass, EVA in the case of solar and tower, nacelle, hub, gear box, etc. in the case of wind can help the local supply eco system develop. The sourcing footprint of these important components is a weak point in the global supply chain, and we see the need to rebalance its geographic spread. Localization could help India become a leader not only in supplies in terms of capacity, but also in technology.

Overall, as we develop manufacturing hubs, we must promote a circular economy concept, creating a more sustainable and resilient supply chain from the design phase to the new models of reusing components at the end of their life cycle. The circular economy offers a new paradigm which is gaining traction at every level and in every geographical setting as a realistic solution that combines market competitiveness and environmental sustainability through innovation. It would mean rethinking production and consumption models to radically reduce the consumption of virgin raw materials and the production of waste. It would encourage using renewable energy sources and materials, extending the useful life of each product, creating sharing platforms, reusing and regenerating, and rethinking products as services.

EDUCATION RECOMMENDATIONS FROM AN EXECUTIVE AT AN AMERICAN SOFTWARE COMPANY

Provide examples for benchmarking education (metrics)

- There needs to be a study providing a data-driven understanding of the actual learning levels of children in schools in India in a range of school systems in different socioeconomic, linguistic, and geographic groups. The focus will also be toward developing frameworks that synthesize the data to recommend performance benchmarks for improvement. Thus, governments will be able to find these benchmarks useful to set program targets and evaluate the change in academic quality across programmes and initiatives in different school categories.

- Until there is a shared understanding at a very specific and detailed level of students' baseline performance in a variety of schools, we cannot meaningfully seek to improve outcomes. There is a need for government initiatives that will help measure, at a broad and unprecedented scale, how children in different school systems, states, and economic circumstances perform. Knowledge developed from these studies should be put to work by policymakers, funders, and other stakeholders to devise programmatic, sustainable, and scalable remedies to the precise challenges identified. These findings should be approached in the spirit of inquiry, of starting a conversation, of sharing knowledge, and of helping Indian children – and India itself – to achieve the greatness of which they are capable.

Identify the weak point(s) of the national education policy.

- According to the India Internet Report 2019, 99% of users in the country access the internet through mobiles, not laptops or computers. Laptop and desktop usage is only 2% and 1% respectively in rural areas and 6% and 4% respectively in urban areas of the country. Further, internet penetration is still very poor and stands at a mere 27% in rural India. Under the Bharat Net Program, more than 40% of the villages have yet to be connected to the internet grid, which creates a disadvantageous situation for rural students.
- Compulsory employability and entrepreneurship-related papers in each semester could promote employability and entrepreneurship among the students. The undergraduate program should be designed to include two skill-based subjects focusing on employability and entrepreneurship skills, apart from core subjects, non-core subjects, and elective subjects. The evaluation scheme for these skill-based subjects should be continuous internal assessment without holding semester end exams. Such an innovative model gives confidence for the students to choose an entrepreneurial career.
- Simplifying patent filing and speedup of patent evaluation: The Indian government, through arranging awareness programmes, can make researchers familiar with patent filing procedures and the patent filing and evaluation fees with the time of evaluation decreased to three to six months instead of the current three to six years. This will encourage innovators to file for patents for their inventions.
- Use of services of retired professors as research guides: We require PhD degree holders in autonomous colleges. Because of changes in policies of NEP 2020, the demand for research guides is increasing. The optimum solution for solving this shortage is to utilize the services of retired

professors with good research experience. Retired professors should be used as research professors irrespective of their age to guide the research scholars in their PhD. This idea will eliminate the scarcity of research guides.

Examine the feasibility of CSR investment into (digital) educational programs.

- In a country like India, which lacks infrastructure support for basic education, digital literacy is a daunting task. Corporates, governments, and NGOs have been devising strategies to bring technology to the doorstep of the rural population. Technology makes learning more hands-on and applicable, thus increasing retention and curiosity among students. CSR programs on holistic educational support (inclusive of digital literacy) for the overall development of the rural community have shown and will continue to show positive results in rural areas where the affordability of basic education itself is a challenge. This encourages students to take up higher education.

- Corporations play a tactical role in bridging the gaps in the current education projects that involve infrastructure support and complement it with the introduction of technology. These projects, in fact, have helped build awareness and self-empowerment of the rural and urban communities by designing modules ranging from basic to advanced IT skills. The telecom and IT sectors have an advantage in terms of supporting digital literacy programs due to their technical expertise in solving last-mile connectivity challenges.

- As part of their CSR mandate, companies can strengthen the digital education program by setting up smart classes or giving infrastructural support to schools in rural and urban areas. There is also scope to join hands with the government and NGOs in their efforts to make the village/panchayat-level functionaries, farmers, youth, and women digitally literate. In addition, corporations can spare their employees who can volunteer to teach computer education and internet services to empower these groups. Corporate-funded technology-driven projects must also include awareness programs that drive behavioral changes and aim to bring down negative rural dynamics to a minimum.

- While corporate funds are being invested in a plethora of activities, spending on improving the education system for rural communities must be continuous. The rural education system can be strengthened with strategic investment by corporations that complement the existing government schemes. Efforts directed to provide accessible educational opportunities will strengthen the capacities of rural youth, resulting in the formation of a useful human resource pool. This will not only help in the growth of rural areas through increased employment opportunities but will also aid the country in its development process.

MOVING FORWARD

"The purpose of a quest is to transform the hero into someone who is capable of achieving the goal."

– Joseph Campbell

THE CONVERSATIONS AND insights captured in these pages reflect the experience and expertise of many wise leaders from the corporate, government, and academic sectors. They suggest some common themes about improving education of the workforce, enhancing the talent pool, and overcoming the barriers of last-mile connectivity.

These improvements will, no doubt, accelerate efforts to restore India's prominence in global manufacturing. But our experience in other areas – such as developing smart villages in Andhra Pradesh and enhancing healthcare in Meghalaya – makes it clear that the principles of open innovation are also an essential part of the recipe for implementing and accelerating change at the kind of scale that will be needed for this quest to succeed.

In an ecosystem based on a foundation of open innovation, change emerges most effectively when ideas are welcome and nurtured from every sector. Political and corporate leaders can often drive change, but change can also emerge from individual entrepreneurs or consumers. Those in roles of power and influence don't hold a monopoly on original ideas, and the shared quest is most effective when there is an ecosystem that invites and nurtures ideas from all sectors. Equally important is ensuring that all sectors proactively share their ideas and their learnings about what's working and what's not working, and strive to understand the reasons why.

How Open Innovation Ecosystems Are Different (and Why That Matters)

The open innovation framework leverages this insight to foster change that emerges from a triple helix model of business innovation. This model incorporates the role of governments, businesses, and research facilities such as universities, and recognizes they can produce more when they work in concert – rather than in siloes.

The characteristics of this kind of open business model include four key features:

- Continuous adaptation to deliver value
- A shift from market places to market "spaces" that aren't constrained by finite physical locations or face-to-face inter-actions or limited hours of operation
- Breaking down internal and external silos, by embracing partnerships within an organization's own structure and within its industry
- Creating or belonging to an ecosystem in which the whole is greater than the sum of the parts and the success of the overall ecosystem takes priority over the success of individual participants in the ecosystem.

Our experience in other projects has consistently shown the importance of the open innovation model for driving changes. This is especially true when those changes involve deeply rooted and nuanced cultural factors, such as strengthening trust across an ecosystem in which different sectors have grown skeptical of one another over the course of many decades.

- With the spirit – and impact – of the open innovation model in mind, we hope that everybody reading these words will recognize the importance of their own role as a vibrant force within the ecosystem that can drive change and bring us forward in the quest to "reset the jewel." With that in mind, we encourage you to contemplate your own answers to the following questions:

- What kind of concrete results would the quest to restore India's global manufacturing prominence yield for you?
- What is your own personal objective related to the quest to "reset the jewel"?
- What steps can you take right now to be part of this initiative?
- What barriers are you aware of that currently prevent you from taking greater steps?
- How could you overcome those barriers?
- Can you think of earlier situations in which similar barriers have been successfully mitigated?
- What people that you know or work with should be part of this initiative?
- Define at least one preliminary goal that will move you closer to your personal objective as well as for the broader national quest.
- What is a reasonable timetable for achieving that preliminary goal? Set yourself a deadline to achieve that result.

Of course, a quest can be a difficult endeavor. And, as the quote from Joseph Campbell that opens this chapter suggests, the real impact that a quest has is on those involved in the quest. While the goal itself may be a worthy outcome, so is the transformation that the quest has on each person who participates in it. To help inspire you on your own role in this quest – and in your own personal transformation – here are a few more quotes you may find helpful in translating the lofty goals of this quest into tangible and actionable steps you can take along your own path toward these goals.

"The purpose of a quest is to find the treasure within you." – Lailah Gifty Akita

"To undertake a quest is to invite struggle into your life. A knight may go on a quest, but it's the battle that makes him a hero." – Peter V. Brett

"The greatest quest in life is to reach one's potential." – Mychal Wynn

"A quest is not always a journey to a far-off place or the search for an elusive prize. It can be a call to challenge yourself, to step out of your comfort zone, and to discover the true extent of your abilities." – Tony Clark

"The quest for certainty blocks the search for meaning. Uncertainty is the very condition to impel man to unfold his powers." – Erich Fromm

"The quest for knowledge and the pursuit of excellence are never-ending journeys, but the rewards are always worth the effort." – Eraldo Banovac

"A quest is not always about achieving a goal. It can be about the journey itself and the experiences and lessons learned along the way." – Unknown

A PERSONAL POSTSCRIPT

Inspirational quotes and theoretical frameworks can only take you so far, however. Ultimately, any significant economic change also needs to harness the power of emotions and relationships among stakeholders. To that end, I'll leave you with two stories from my personal experience, one about the impact of trust and the other about importance of values.

A STORY ON TRUST

TRUST GENERATES A strong and sustainable economy.

While I was growing up in India in the late sixties, my father was doing his post-doctoral work at UC San Diego. He wrote many letters describing the greatness of America and sent pictures to support his claim. I distinctly remember several pictures of roadside shops with priced products left unattended. Often the cash register was just a small basket where money was deposited, and change was taken by the customers. The owners came by at the end of the day to collect the cash. Today, such shops no longer exist in San Diego. Something has changed over the course of time. Our society is no less affluent, at present, than in the late sixties; the change in business practice is not correlated with economic prosperity. It is worth exploring the causes for the abdication of values that we had once in our society.

My friend, Vishal Mangalwadi, an Indian social activist, author, and philosopher, told me about an experience he had while visiting Holland in the late eighties. During his visit, his host took him on a short walk to buy milk at the dairy. Vishal had never seen so many cows in their stalls, unattended, automatically milked. There was no one taking inventory or attending the cash register. The milk was automatically drained from the cows into a large container. His host simply opened the tap, filled his bottle, and pulled out his coins, which he put into a basket from which he also collected the right amount of change. As they were walking back, Vishal remarked, "If I were in India, I would take both the milk and the money."

You see, if customers are not honest, the owner needs to hire a salesclerk. And, if the customers are not honest, why do the sales-clerk and the owners need to be honest? They would just add water to the milk. When the owner is not honest, the customers complain, which means inspectors need to be hired.

But if the customers, salesforce, and owners cheat, why should the inspectors be honest? They will want bribes. Then, an organization like the US's Public Company Accounting Oversight Board (PCAOB), the Financial Accounting Standards Board (FASB), and the Securities and Exchange Commission (SEC) are needed to oversee their work. Additional monitoring costs for salesclerks, inspectors, and PCAOB are then passed on to the consumer. Who will pay for all the additional costs – the salesclerks, the inspectors, and the bribes? Of course, the customer/taxpayer will. Soon, the milk sold in India would be far more expensive than milk sold in Holland and Indian parents will not be able to afford milk for their children. The children of India, the nation's future workforce and economic engine, would be more malnourished than those in Holland. On his plane back, Vishal, sat next to an Indian businessman who spoke little English, but was able to run prosperous businesses here in the West. He remarked to Vishal that doing business in America and England is much easier because you can trust people there. The values held in the West, he said, are more conducive to doing business than in India where corruption reigns at all levels.

These stories illustrate some of the predicaments we are faced with today.

I was a corporate officer for over 14 years before I entered academia. I still think we could do a better job of instilling in our workforce ethics and values to promote social and personal responsibility. We are so busy running our shops that we neglect to invest in training or seminars to address these foundational issues. Prevention is better than cure. It is my conviction that our society will continue to pay a high cost for our products unless we address the root of the problem. At our Annual Conference on Financial Reporting in

Berkeley, we were fortunate to have with us board members, senior officers, and executives representing the regulatory and standard-setting boards, major corporations, accounting firms, and professional associations.

When I was in college, we did not have as many organizations overseeing the profession. My accounting professor told me that the profession is "self-regulated" – a noble concept. That was not that long ago. Today things are more expensive because we have the police policing the police.

Corporations in America today are realizing that our economic engine is powered by ethics and values that promote social and personal responsibility – a concept which has been neglected for some time. American corporations are now placing more importance on values that serve as the foundation to their mission statements.

Our young people are being trained in business schools that have incorporated ethics into their curricula. This is a good direction, but we still have a way to go. At our conference, as we engaged in dialogues with the standards-setters, regulators, practitioners and academicians, we addressed our problems, but only in part.

All across this nation, at conferences such as these, we wrestle with the consequences of actions – the branches, but not the root, of the problem. After leaving the conference and returning to their places of work, corporate officers still need to address problems having to do with ethical behavior in the workplace. They may leave the conference with knowledge of the various technical agendas to address our problems, but they are still not equipped to address some of the root causes.

Ralph Larsen, former chairman and CEO of Johnson & Johnson said it best: "The core values embodied in our Mission Statement might be a competitive advantage, but that is not why we have them. We have them because they define for us what we stand for, and we would hold them even if they became a competitive disadvantage." Here he simply states that his company will not compromise its values even if profitability suffers. To me, that is a strong foundation for good financial reporting.

A STORY ON VALUES

Values are what are needed to generate an environment of trust.

Over thirty years ago I sat at a table graced by a highly regarded religious scholar, Dr. Ralph Winter, and his dear wife for breakfast in Pasadena at the US Center for World Missions which he founded. Over the course of our discussion, Mrs. Winter told a story based on her research about bloodthirsty Vikings of Norway that I had long forgotten. A few years ago, I was invited by Norwegian Business School to give a series of lectures. It was during this first-time visit that the story Mrs. Winter told all came back to me.

The point of her story was that Vikings who raided other neighboring countries in Europe would not only kill people, but they brought many beautiful women home against their will. The women who were stolen and separated from their families held moral values far different than their new Viking husbands. The Christian women, instead of taking revenge and being bitter they lived by the moral values they held dear in their hearts and operated on the principle that Christ taught in Matthew 5:43-48: "Ye have heard that it hath been said, thou shalt love thy neighbor, and hate thine enemy. But I say unto you, Love your enemies, bless them that curse you, do good to them that hate you, and pray for them which despitefully use you, and persecute you; That ye may be the children of your Father which is in heaven: for he maketh his sun to rise on the evil and on the good, and sendeth rain on the just and on the unjust. For if ye love them which love you, what reward have ye? do not even the publicans the same? And if ye salute your brethren only, what do ye more than others? do not even the publicans so? Be ye therefore perfect, even as your Father which is in heaven is perfect." Because of the testimony of these people who were persecuted for their faith, the Viking men changed their behaviors and adopted Christian faith over time.

When I arrived in Norway years later after hearing this story, I saw a church on every corner. I saw in public as well as private places where payment needs to be made, I saw no cashier there to collect cash – it was all on an honor system where people put money in the bucket and took the right amount of change back.

How could this be? How could once-bloodthirsty savages who stole, raped, and destroyed families establish a nation where there is little or no crime. A nation was transformed over time by values held dear by women in captivity.

I used to be a forensic accounting teacher and developed curricula for accounting fraud courses both at USC and Berkeley. I also served as an expert witness in court hearings. Due to my background, I was sought out by the Office of the Comptroller Auditor General of India to teach courses in accounting fraud. Two years ago, I was invited by the comptroller and auditor general of India to advise on curriculum for teaching and training his supreme audit institution of India to curtail corruption in his country. Following my presentation to his group that listened to me virtually nationwide, he said our nation operates on "distrust" and not on "trust."

That prompted me to reflect on how much the faith-based values held by a nation can drive a healthy economy. If there was hope for the Viking nation, there is hope for India.

EPILOGUE:
TRUST STARTS FROM THE TOP

*"The people when rightly and
fully trusted will return the trust."*

– Abraham Lincoln

AS MENTIONED EARLIER, the "aha" insight that sparked this book came during a meeting with Prime Minister Narendra Modi, when he was confronted with a question about the lack of trust among stakeholder groups inside India. Whereas earlier administrations had other issues to contend with – Nehru had focused on building up the country's leadership in innovation and technology, for example – re-establishing the bonds of trust should be Modi's first priority. Rather than focusing on the Indian Institutes of Technology, the suggestion was that Modi should focus his energies on something even more fundamental, something one might call an Indian Institute of Trust.

That was when I realized that it would be a steep uphill climb to motivate foreign investment in India – which would require external stakeholders to trust their Indian counterparts – if we didn't have adequate levels of trust among internal stakeholder groups.

To be clear, this erosion of trust predates Prime Minister Modi's tenure. And Mr. Modi identifies himself in a manner that bodes well for the restoration of greater levels of trust among internal stakeholders. He considers himself to be a servant of the people, or a "pradhan sewak." As he told the nation at his first Independence Day address in 2014: "My beloved countrymen! I have come here not as a 'pradhan mantri' (prime minister) but a 'pradhan sewak' (prime servant)."

Throughout world history, servant leadership has played a crucial role in creating or rebuilding trust in civilizations and nations in which trust had crumbled. The U.S. President Abraham Lincoln was one such leader, listening closely to the needs of a broken nation.

Indeed, many of the world's great leaders across history – many of them coming at particularly challenging moments in world history – have considered themselves to be (and demonstrated themselves to be) servant leaders. Here are just a few of these leaders (from different eras, different parts of the globe, and different spheres of influence) and the way they've characterized their own philosophies as servant leaders:

"Here I am among you as one who serves. I have come not to be served but to serve"– **Jesus Christ**

"If you light a lamp for somebody, it will also brighten your path." – **Gautama Buddha**

"Once you start working on something, don't be afraid of failure and don't abandon it. People who work sincerely are the happiest." – **Chanakya**

"With the right attitude, self-imposed limitations vanish." – **Alexander the Great**

"Let he who would move the world first move himself." – **Socrates**

"I suppose leadership at one time meant muscles; but today it means getting along with people." – **Mahatma Gandhi**

"It is high time the ideal of success should be replaced with the ideal of service." – **Albert Einstein**

"The first responsibility of a leader is to define reality. The last is to say thank you. In between, the leader is a servant." – **Max De Pree**

"As we look ahead into the next century, leaders will be those who empower others." – **Bill Gates**

This concept of servant leadership relates to this book in two significant ways. First, the premise of the book – that rebuilding India as a leader in the global economy requires first rebuilding trust within our own borders – is a concept that falls within the purview of servant leadership. You can't bully your way into a trusting relationship; you have to earn it, through your words, actions, and your willingness to engage in robust dialogue with other stakeholders.

And second, the trajectory of this book itself reflects the authors' philosophy of servant leadership. We may have our own ideas about what's most important for India to rebuild its prominence in the global economy, but we readily acknowledge that we certainly don't have all the answers. What we do have is the ability and willingness to ask questions.

So this book is merely the first step in the roadmap to rebuilding India, and resetting the jewel in the crown (even if the "crown" itself has faded in its luster).

We look forward to continuing this process of discovery with you as your servant leaders in this journey.

APPENDIX 1:
BIFI Participants — Rebuilding India Initiative
August, 2020

	Company Name	Name of Executive	Designation
1	Adobe India	Abhigyan Modi	Country Manager
2	AIMA	Rekha Sethi	Director General
3	Apollo Hospitals	Preetha Reddy	Vice-Chairperson
4	Applied Materials India	Srinivas Satya	President
5	Autodesk India	Rajeev Mittal	Managing Director
6	Avery Dennison	Pradeep Iyer	Senior Global Director
7	AWS India	Rahul Sharma	President
8	AWS India	Manav Seghal	Head of National Cloud Innovation
9	Dell India	Alok Ohrie	President
10	Dr. Reddy's Labs	Satish Reddy	Chairman
11	Enel Green Power India	Sandy Khera	Country Manager & CEO
12	Ericsson, Silicon Valley	Mallik Tatipamula	CTO
13	HDFC Securities	Dhiraj Relli	Managing Director & CEO
14	Hero Cycles	Pankaj Munjal	Chairman
15	Hero Enterprise	Sunil Munjal	Chairman
16	IBM India	Sandip Patel	Managing Director
17	Infosys	Nandan Nilekani	Co-Founder & Non-Ex Chairman
18	Intel India	Nivruti Rai	Country Head
19	Reliance Jio	Raghuram Lanka	Head, Digital Healthcare
20	Johnson Controls, APAC	Visal Leng	President
21	Kirloskar	Sanjay Kirloskar	Chairman
22	Manipal Global Education	T.V.Mohandas Pai	Chairman
23	Manipal Hospitals Group	Sudarshan Ballal	Chairman
24	Microsoft India	Anant Maheshwari	President
25	NITI Aayog	Amitabh Kant	CEO
26	NPCI	Dilip Asbe	Managing Director & CEO

27	Nvidia	Pyush Modi	Chief Strategist, Industrial Sector
28	Nvidia, South Asia	Vishal Dhupar	Managing Director
29	Reliance	R. Venkat	Advisor
30	Reliance Industries	Nikhil Meswani	Executive Director, Board of Directors
31	Reliance Jio	Prateek Pashine	President
32	Salesforce	Charlie Isaacs	CTO, Customer Success
33	Salesforce India	Arundhati Bhattacharya	Chairman & CEO
34	SAP Labs India	Sindhu Gangadharan	Managing Director & SVP
35	Smart Village Movement	Anil Shah	Chairman
36	Tata Chemicals	R. Mukundan	CEO
37	Tata Power	Dr. Praveer Sinha	CEO
38	TechMahindra	CP Gurnani	CEO
39	Thyssenkrupp India	Ravi Kirpalani	Managing Director & CEO
40	VMware	Pradeep Nair	Managing Director
41	VMware	Sanjay Poonan	COO
42	Wipro	Sanjeev Singh	Head of Business
43	Wipro Global	K R Sanjiv	CTO
44	Xerox	Santokh Badesha	Chief Scientist

APPENDIX 2:

2022 Berkeley Innovation Forum India Participants

CEOs, CTOs, and other senior leaders from the following global firms and government organizations participated in the 2022 BIF-India.

1. Adobe
2. Apollo Hospitals
3. Autodesk
4. Amazon
5. Coca Cola
6. Dell
7. Dr. Reddy Labs
8. Ericsson
9. Hero Cycles
10. Hero Enterprises
11. IBM
12. Indian Embassy of US
13. Infosys
14. Intel
15. Intex Technologies
16. Microsoft
17. NASA
18. Nestle
19. The NITI Aayog
20. Nvidia
21. PayTM
22. Petonics Infotech
23. Reliance Industries
24. Reliance Jio
25. Salesforce
26. SAP

27. Stashrun
28. TATA Chemicals
29. TATA Power
30. TechMahindra
31. Thyssenkrupp
32. Unilever
33. Wipro
34. Xerox

APPENDIX 3: SOURCES

1. https://www.dailypioneer.com/2020/columnists/rethink-logistics-logically.html
2. https://razorpay.com/blog/why-do-refunds-take-time/
3. https://www.business-standard.com/article/economy-policy/india-inc-spent-more-on-r-d-in-fy19-auto-and-pharma-leadingsectors-119103100062_1.html
4. https://www.thehindu.com/news/national/kerala/delayed-justice-from-consumer-courts/article28662030.ece
5. https://www.dailypioneer.com/2020/columnists/rethink-logistics-logically.html
6. https://www.careratings.com/upload/NewsFiles/Studies/Warehousing%20Industry%20October%202018.pdf
7. https://www.indiatoday.in/education-today/featurephilia/story/why-33-of-formally-trained-youth-remained-unemployedin-2017-18-alone-need-for-skill-development-1599153-2019-09-23
8. https://inc42.com/datalab/human-capital-is-india-biggest-strength-but-lack-of-rd-spending-hurts-innovation/
9. https://www.livemint.com/budget/economic-survey/it-s-easier-doing-business-in-india-now-but-starting-up-is-still-hardto-do-11580492222123.html
10. https://www.financialexpress.com/economy/a-wishlist-of-top-five-direct-tax-reforms-to-boost-indias-economic-health/2008863/
11. https://www.dailypioneer.com/2020/columnists/rethink-logistics-logically.html
12. https://www.thebalance.com/india-s-economy-3306348
13. https://www.indiatoday.in/education-today/featurephilia/story/why-33-of-formally-trained-youth-remained-unemployedin-2017-18-alone-need-for-skill-development-1599153-2019-09-23
14. https://www.forbes.com/sites/theyec/2011/12/14/3-reasons-toask-for-customer-feedback/?sh=6a5699304700

15. https://www.careratings.com/upload/NewsFiles/Studies/Ware-housing%20Industry%20October%202018.pdf

16. https://consumerhelpline.gov.in/

17. https://www.thehindu.com/news/national/kerala/delayed-jus-tice-from-consumer-courts/article28662030.ece

18. https://www.dailypioneer.com/2020/columnists/rethink-logis-tics-logically.html

19. https://www.financialexpress.com/economy/a-wishlist-of-top-fivedirect-tax-reforms-to-boost-indias-economic-health/2008863/

20. https://www.thehindu.com/news/national/8000-cases-pending-for-over-5-years-in-labour-courts-tribunals/article32661996.ece

21. https://inc42.com/datalab/human-capital-is-india-biggest-strength-but-lack-of-rd-spending-hurts-innovation

22. https://www.indiatoday.in/education-today/featurephilia/story/why-33-of-formally-trained-youth-remained-unemployedin-2017-18-alone-need-for-skill-development-1599153-2019-09-23

23. https://www.thehindu.com/business/Industry/why-indian-firms-dont-innovate/article23474524.ece

24. https://www.indiatoday.in/education-today/featurephilia/story/why-33-of-formally-trained-youth-remained-unemployedin-2017-18-alone-need-for-skill-development-1599153-2019-09-23

25. https://inc42.com/datalab/human-capital-is-india-biggest-strength-but-lack-of-rd-spending-hurts-innovation/

26. https://www.thebalance.com/india-s-economy-3306348

27. https://www.indiatoday.in/education-today/featurephilia/story/why-33-of-formally-trained-youth-remained-unemployedin-2017-18-alone-need-for-skill-development-1599153-2019-09-23

28. https://inc42.com/datalab/human-capital-is-india-biggest-strength-but-lack-of-rd-spending-hurts-innovation

29. https://www2.deloitte.com/ca/en/pages/consumer-business/arti-cles/consumer-driven-innovation.html

30. https://www2.deloitte.com/content/dam/Deloitte/in/Documents/public-sector/in-ps-india-on-cusp-of-a-logistics-revolution-noexp.pdf

31. https://www.careratings.com/upload/NewsFiles/Studies/Warehousing%20Industry%20October%202018.pdf

32. https://www.forbes.com/sites/henrychesbrough/2011/03/21/everything-you-need-to-know-about-open-innovation/?sh=5215c0d675f4

33. https://economictimes.indiatimes.com/small-biz/trade/exports/logistics/india-can-add-8-to-its-exports-if-it-puts-its-last-mile-connect-in-the-fast-lane/articleshow/70782149.cms?from=mdr

34. https://www.outlookindia.com/blog/story/india-news-india-lacksinnovation-if-you-dont-believe-it-just-look-at-who-domina/4109

35. https://www.google.com/url?sa=t&rct=j&q=&esrc=s&source=web&cd=&ved=2ahUKEwjVgIKhvc3tAhXI4jgGHQk5DzYQFjACegQIAhAC&url=http%3A%2F%2Fwww.informaticsjournals.com%2Findex.php%2Fdbijb%2Farticle%2Fdownload%2F16072%2F13471&usg=AOvVaw1RQohEfSQjhyHkilj4rj3N

36. https://www.thehindu.com/business/Industry/why-indian-firms-dont-innovate/article23474524.ece

37. http://iec.edu.in/blog/digital-india-opportunities-challenges/#:~:text=There%20are%20many%20roadblocks%20in,full%20potential%20of%20this%20programme.

38. https://www.thehindu.com/business/Industry/why-indian-firms-dont-innovate/article23474524.ece

39. https://nasscom.in/sites/default/files/Wipro_NASSCOM_OI_for_New_World_of_Tomorrow_POV.PDF

40. https://www.devalt.org/newsletter/jul19/lead.htm

41. https://inc42.com/resources/product-innovation-gap-indian-companies-make-for-india/

42. https://www.mckinsey.com/business-functions/mckinsey-digital/ourinsights/digital-india-technology-to-transform-a-connected-nation#

43. https://www.thehindu.com/business/Industry/why-indian-firms-dont-innovate/article23474524.ece

44. https://www.consultantsreview.com/cxoinsights/challenges-facing-the-indian-market-research-industry-vid-731.html

45. https://inc42.com/resources/product-innovation-gap-indian-companies-make-for-india/

46. https://www.indiatoday.in/education-today/featurephilia/story/why-33-of-formally-trained-youth-remained-unemployedin-2017-18-alone-need-for-skill-development-1599153-2019-09-23

47. https://www.thebalance.com/india-s-economy-3306348

48. https://inc42.com/resources/product-innovation-gap-indian-companies-make-for-india/

49. https://www.forbes.com/sites/theyec/2011/12/14/3-reasons-toask-for-customer-feedback/?sh=6a5699304700

50. https://www.livemint.com/budget/economic-survey/it-s-easier-doing-business-in-india-now-but-starting-up-is-still-hardto-do-11580492222123.html

51. https://www.dailypioneer.com/2020/columnists/rethink-logistics-logically.html

52. https://www.thebalance.com/india-s-economy-3306348

53. https://www.indiatoday.in/education-today/featurephilia/story/why-33-of-formally-trained-youth-remained-unemployedin-2017-18-alone-need-for-skill-development-1599153-2019-09-23

54. https://www.financialexpress.com/industry/sme/msme-techsmall-business-technology-msme-cloud-adoption-digital-technology-india-sme-forum-intel-india/1770091/

55. https://www.dailypioneer.com/2020/columnists/rethink-logistics-logically.html

56. https://www.thedollarbusiness.com/magazine/warehousing-inindia---changing-gears-to-meet-future-challenges/31043

57. https://indianexpress.com/article/opinion/columns/the-problem-of-skilling-india-unemployment-joblessness-modi-government-5973808/

58. https://m.economictimes.com/news/economy/policy/inadequate-enforcement-and-lack-of-consumer-awareness-boostingcounterfeiting-in-india-ficci/articleshow/50590384.cms

59.   https://www.business-standard.com/article/economy-policy/
       india-inc-spent-more-on-r-d-in-fy19-auto-and-pharma-leadingsec-
       tors-119103100062_1.html

60.   https://www.thehindu.com/business/Industry/why-indian-firms-
       dont-innovate/article23474524.ece

61.   https://www.forbes.com/sites/theyec/2011/12/14/3-reasons-
       toask-for-customer-feedback/?sh=6a5699304700

62.   https://www.livemint.com/budget/economic-survey/it-s-easier-
       doing-business-in-india-now-but-starting-up-is-still-hardto-do-
       11580492222123.html

63.   https://www.dailypioneer.com/2020/columnists/rethink-logis-
       tics-logically.html

64.   https://inc42.com/resources/product-innovation-gap-indian-
       companies-make-for-india/

65.   https://www.financialexpress.com/industry/sme/msme-techsmall-
       business-technology-msme-cloud-adoption-digital-technology-
       india-sme-forum-intel-india/1770091/

66.   https://www.thebalance.com/india-s-economy-3306348

67.   https://www.timesnownews.com/india/article/environmentale-
       vil-causes-of-industrial-pollution-and-ways-to-control-it/670919

68.   https://www.prnewswire.com/news-releases/the-logistics-market-
       inindia-2020---growth-opportunities-latest-government-regulations-
       keystart-ups-major-challenges-disruptive-innovations-301034835.html

69.   https://www.thedollarbusiness.com/magazine/warehousing-inin-
       dia---changing-gears-to-meet-future-challenges/31043

70.   https://www.ies.gov.in/pdfs/Problems_of_MSME.pdf

71.   https://www.forbes.com/sites/jeffboss/2016/04/26/
       staying-competitive-requires-adaptability/?sh=577d26b97e6f

72.   https://www.thehindu.com/business/Industry/why-indian-firms-
       dont-innovate/article23474524.ece

73.   **https**://www.indiatoday.in/education-today/featurephilia/story/why-
       33-of-formally-trained-youth-remained-unemployedin-2017-18-alone-
       need-for-skill-development-1599153-2019-09-23

74.   https://www.devalt.org/newsletter/jul19/lead.htm

75.   https://www.mckinsey.com/business-functions/mckinsey-dig-ital/our-insights/digital-india-technology-to-transform-a-con-nected-nation#

76.   https://inc42.com/datalab/human-capital-is-india-biggest-strength-but-lack-of-rd-spending-hurts-innovation

77.   https://www.indiatoday.in/education-today/featurephilia/story/why-33-of-formally-trained-youth-remained-unemployedin-2017-18-alone-need-for-skill-development-1599153-2019-09-23

78.   https://www.jigsawacademy.com/cyber-security-challengesin-india/

79.   https://www.thehindu.com/business/Industry/why-indian-firms-dont-innovate/article23474524.ece

80.   https://www.financialexpress.com/opinion/explainedwhy-indias-productivity-is-low-and-cost-of-production-highchina/2005499/

81.   https://www.thedollarbusiness.com/magazine/warehousing-inin-dia---changing-gears-to-meet-future-challenges/31043

82.   **https**://www.dailypioneer.com/2020/columnists/rethink-logis-tics-logically.html

83.   **https**://www.dailypioneer.com/2020/columnists/rethink-logis-tics-logically.html

84.   https://indianexpress.com/article/opinion/columns/the-prob-lem-of-skilling-india-unemployment-joblessness-modi-govern-ment-5973808/

85.   https://www.business-standard.com/article/economy-policy/india-inc-spent-more-on-r-d-in-fy19-auto-and-pharma-leadingsec-tors-119103100062_1.html

86.   https://www.dailypioneer.com/2020/columnists/rethink-logis-tics-logically.html

87.   https://www.livemint.com/budget/economic-survey/it-s-easier-doing-business-in-india-now-but-starting-up-is-still-hardto-do-11580492222123.html

88. https://inc42.com/resources/product-innovation-gap-indian-companies-make-for-india/
89. https://www.indiatoday.in/education-today/featurephilia/story/why-33-of-formally-trained-youth-remained-unemployedin-2017-18-alone-need-for-skill-development-1599153-2019-09-23
90. https://www.indiansmechamber.com/challenges_to_msme.php
91. https://inc42.com/resources/product-innovation-gap-indian-companies-make-for-india/
92. https://inc42.com/datalab/human-capital-is-india-biggest-strength-but-lack-of-rd-spending-hurts-innovation
93. https://www.indiansmechamber.com/challenges_to_msme.php
94. https://www.insightssuccess.in/opportunities-challenges-indian manufacturing-industry
95. https://www.forbes.com/sites/theyec/2011/12/14/3-reasons-toask-for-customer-feedback/?sh=6a5699304700
96. https://www.eai.in/ref/ae/wte/typ/clas/india_industrial_wastes.html
97. https://www.financialexpress.com/industry/sme/msme-techsmall-business-technology-msme-cloud-adoption-digital-technology-india-sme-forum-intel-india/1770091/
98. https://www.devalt.org/newsletter/jul19/lead.htm
99. https://www.financialexpress.com/industry/sme/msme-techsmall-business-technology-msme-cloud-adoption-digital-technology-india-sme-forum-intel-india/1770091/
100. https://inc42.com/datalab/human-capital-is-india-biggest-strength-but-lack-of-rd-spending-hurts-innovation
101. https://www2.deloitte.com/ca/en/pages/consumer-business/articles/consumer-driven-innovation.html
102. https://www.financialexpress.com/opinion/explained-why-indias-productivity-is-low-and-cost-of-production-high-china/2005499/
103. https://indianexpress.com/article/opinion/columns/the-problem-of-skilling-india-unemployment-joblessness-modi-government-5973808/

104. https://www.business-standard.com/article/economy-policy/india-inc-spent-more-on-r-d-in-fy19-auto-and-pharma-leadingsectors-119103100062_1.html
105. https://www2.deloitte.com/ca/en/pages/consumer-business/articles/consumer-driven-innovation.html
106. https://www.dailypioneer.com/2020/columnists/rethink-logistics-logically.html
107. https://www.financialexpress.com/industry/msme-fin-governments-financial-package-for-msmes-liquidity-credit-challengefor-small-businesses/1955031/
108. https://www.livemint.com/budget/economic-survey/it-s-easier-doing-business-in-india-now-but-starting-up-is-still-hardto-do-11580492222123.html
109. https://inc42.com/resources/product-innovation-gap-indian-companies-make-for-india/
110. https://cio.economictimes.indiatimes.com/news/next-gen-technologies/can-smart-factories-help-india-become-a-global-manufacturing-hub/74821115
111. https://www.forbes.com/sites/theyec/2011/12/14/3-reasons-toask-for-customer-feedback/?sh=6a5699304700
112. https://www.business-standard.com/article/economy-policy/despite-make-in-india-push-industry-share-in-gdp-hit-20-year-low-in-2019-120111801618_1.html
113. https://inc42.com/datalab/human-capital-is-india-biggest-strength-but-lack-of-rd-spending-hurts-innovation
114. https://inc42.com/datalab/human-capital-is-india-biggest-strength-but-lack-of-rd-spending-hurts-innovation
115. https://www.indiatoday.in/education-today/featurephilia/story/why-33-of-formally-trained-youth-remained-unemployedin-2017-18-alone-need-for-skill-development-1599153-2019-09-23
116. https://www.thehindu.com/business/Industry/why-indian-firms-dont-innovate/article23474524.ece

117. https://indianexpress.com/article/opinion/columns/the-problem-of-skilling-india-unemployment-joblessness-modi-government-5973808/

118. https://m.economictimes.com/news/economy/policy/inadequate-enforcement-and-lack-of-consumer-awareness-boostingcounterfeiting-in-india-ficci/articleshow/50590384.cms

119. https://inc42.com/resources/product-innovation-gap-indian-companies-make-for-india/

120. https://cio.economictimes.indiatimes.com/news/next-gen-technologies/can-smart-factories-help-india-become-a-global-manufacturing-hub/74821115

121. https://www.indiatoday.in/education-today/featurephilia/story/why-33-of-formally-trained-youth-remained-unemployedin-2017-18-alone-need-for-skill-development-1599153-2019-09-23

APPENDIX 4:
Summary of 2022 Berkeley Innovation Forum

A password-protected white paper summarizing the proceedings of the 2022 Berkeley Innovation Forum held in India can be found at https://growthmarkets.berkeley.edu/bifi-white-paper-2022.

To request access to the white paper, email sdarwin@berkeley.edu briefly explaining your interest and professional affiliations.

OTHER BOOKS
BY PROFESSOR SOLOMON DARWIN

https://www.amazon.com/stores/Solomon-Darwin/author/
B08CMP2F3P

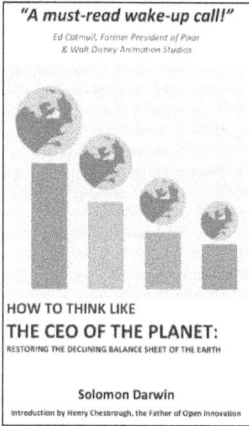

"A must-read wake-up call!"

Ed Catmull, Former President of Pixar
& Walt Disney Animation Studios

HOW TO THINK LIKE
THE CEO OF THE PLANET:
RESTORING THE DECLINING BALANCE SHEET OF THE EARTH

Solomon Darwin

Introduction by Henry Chesbrough, the Father of Open Innovation

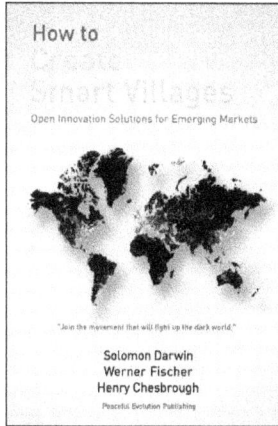

How to
Create
Smart Villages

Open Innovation Solutions for Emerging Markets

"Join the movement that will light up the dark world."

Solomon Darwin
Werner Fischer
Henry Chesbrough

Peaceful Evolution Publishing

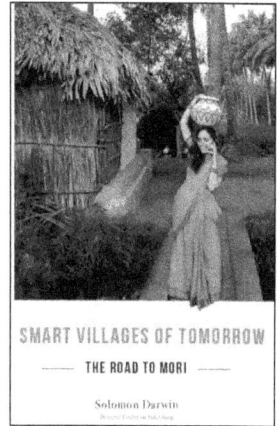

SMART VILLAGES OF TOMORROW

THE ROAD TO MORI

Solomon Darwin

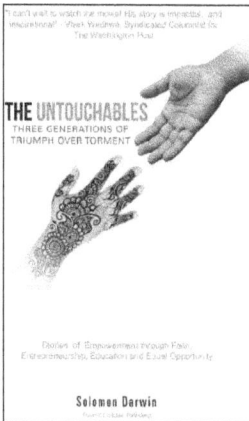

THE UNTOUCHABLES
THREE GENERATIONS OF
TRIUMPH OVER TORMENT

Solomon Darwin

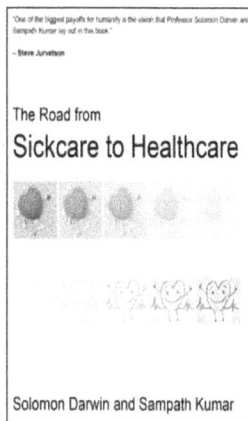

The Road from
Sickcare to Healthcare

Solomon Darwin and Sampath Kumar

9 781736 714607